If you find this book, either
enjoy it yourself or return to...

_____

_____

_____

_____

AN INTERACTIVE BIBLE STUDY BY

MARGARET FEINBERG

scouting the divine

SEARCHING FOR GOD IN WINE, WOOL, AND WILD HONEY

Published by LifeWay Press®
© 2010 Margaret Feinberg
Reprinted May 2014

ISBN: 978-1-4158-6835-5
Item: 005258265

Dewey decimal classification number: 248.83
Subject heading: SPIRITUAL LIFE \ GOD—BIBLICAL TEACHING

Printed in the United States of America.

Young Adult Ministry Publishing
LifeWay Church Resources
One LifeWay Plaza
Nashville, Tennessee 37234-0152

We believe the Bible has God for its author; salvation for its end; and truth,
without any mixture of error, for its matter and that all Scripture is totally true
and trustworthy. To review LifeWay's doctrinal guideline, please visit *www.
lifeway.com/doctrinalguideline.*

All Scripture quotations are taken from the New American Standard Bible,
Copyright © 1960, 1962, 1963, 1968, 1971, 1972, 1973, 1975, 1977, 1995 by the
Lockman Foundation. Used by permission. *(www.lockman.org)*

Cover design by Micah Kandros Design.

TABLE OF CONTENTS

MEET THE AUTHOR
MARGARET FEINBERG

A self-described "hot mess," Margaret Feinberg is a popular Bible teacher and speaker at churches and leading conferences such as Catalyst, Thrive, and Women of Joy, and creator of best-selling coloring books for grown ups—*Live Loved: An Adult Coloring Book* and *Live Free: An Adult Coloring Book*. Her books, including *The Organic God*, *The Sacred Echo*, *Scouting the Divine*, *Wonderstruck*, *Fight Back With Joy*, and their corresponding Bible studies, have sold nearly one million copies and received critical acclaim and extensive national media coverage from CNN, the Associated Press, USA Today, Los Angeles Times, Washington Post, and more.

She was recently named one of 50 women most shaping culture and the church today by Christianity Today, one of the 30 Voices who will help lead the church in the next decade by Charisma magazine and one of 40 who will shape Christian publishing by Christian Retailing magazine. Margaret lives in Salt Lake City, Utah with her husband, Leif, and their superpup, Hershey. She believes some of the best days are spent in jammies, laughing, and being silly.

If you want to put a smile on Margaret's face, write her:
   hello@margaretfeinberg.com

margaretfeinberg.com
facebook.com/margaretfeinberg
twitter.com/mafeinberg
instagram.com/mafeinberg

scouting the divine

INTRODUCTION
THE WONDER OF GOD'S WORD

While some dismiss the Bible as a dusty old book, I tend to view the pages as portals to the adventure of a lifetime. Not only are the passages chock-full of clever plots, compelling stories, and unforgettable characters, they're laced with historical insights and literary beauty. When I open my well-worn leather Bible, I imagine myself walking into an ancient kingdom. As I cross into this foreign land, I imagine a castle with too many banquet halls and bedrooms to count—secret hallways, underground passages, and trap doors abound for the most inquisitive visitors.

> THROUGH CONVERSATIONS AND INTERACTIONS IN WARM LIVING ROOMS AND WET FIELDS, I EXPERIENCED SCRIPTURE IN A WAY I NEVER HAD.

With every turn, I find myself in the presence of kings and queens, princes and prophets, pilgrims and poets sharing their stories of courage and faith. With every encounter, I learn something new about their life journeys. Some of their stories are downright despicable and shockingly frank. Others are simply remarkable: Men who wrestled with lions and bears, women and children who saved nations, and an Unforgettable who chose death so we could live.

The more time I spend in this ancient kingdom, the more I notice that every person's story—even the most unexpected ones—tells the greater story of God and His unabashed love of humanity. With time, I'm learning about their internal struggles, the unimaginable hardships, and the unexpected parallels to my own story that emerge as they follow God. With every morsel of discovery, something inside of me comes alive.

Closing my Bible, I often find the stories haunt me. Sometimes it's a single phrase or sentence or someone in the narrative I had noticed before but never really taken time to get to know. On rare occasions I stumble upon a rich life lesson that transforms me forever.

Now there are plenty of days I try to enter this ancient kingdom and only feel the distance between that world and my own. Instead of riveting stories, I find the accounts flat, stiff, even dull. In quiet misery I shut the book, secretly hoping, even praying, that next time will be better. Sometimes those days run into weeks and months as if the trapdoors have been nailed shut, the banquet hall emptied, not a scrap of conversation or sustenance to be found. Then quite unexpectedly I'll return, and once again the kingdom is alive, full, and overflowing. What's the difference? Maybe it's me. I don't know.

But I suspect that Lucy from C. S. Lewis' *The Lion, the Witch and the Wardrobe* shared similar feelings when she discovered the door at the back of the wardrobe permanently closed. Like Lucy, I'm constantly waiting for winks in time when the portal opens and I can experience the vibrancy of a world that at times seems far more real than my own.

WHEN THE PROPHETS—INCLUDING JESUS—SPOKE OF SHEEP & SHEPHERDS, BEES & HONEY, FIELDS & HARVESTS, GRAPES AND VINES, LISTENERS UNDERSTOOD THEIR REFERENCES IN WAYS THAT I SIMPLY DON'T.

Sometimes those flashes come in response to a simple prayer, *God, help me see You,* or during an extended time of reflection and study. Often they appear while mining through commentaries, translations, ancient word meanings, and even history books in an effort to touch the texture of the text. Occasionally they occur when a particular theme of Scripture is unexpectedly illuminated during a conversation, a film, or an art exhibit. But with every luminescent moment of discovery, I find myself hungering for more.

Why? Because I have this hunch that when aged Scriptures come alive in our contemporary hearts, they don't inform us as much as they transform us. When the good Book connects to our world and envelops our lives, our attitudes, actions, and behaviors change. We become more than good people, we become godly ones who can't help but walk, talk, and live differently. I ache for those instances when promises and teachings from long ago crystallize in spiritual awakening.

Scouting the Divine is a personal spiritual pilgrimage to understand portions of the story of God that I've never understood before. It's an intentional search to move from just reading the Bible to being ushered into the story—one that can be touched, tasted, heard, seen, and smelled. I want to experience the life that is inherent in the Bible in such a way that it deepens my faith in God and my hope for that which is still to come. In some ways, I think we're all "Scouting the Divine"—looking for ways in which God intersects our world in vibrant expressions.

Interestingly, my own journey began nearly a decade ago in a distant land long before I ever realized I had taken the first step or knew where I was going—but then again, that's often how the best ones begin. My pilgrimage began with a shepherdess I met during my first summer in Alaska. The next thing I knew I was in southern Colorado with a passionate, hardworking beekeeper. Then I was on my way to Nebraska to walk the fields with a farmer's nephew. Soon after, I traveled to California to listen and learn about vines from a veteran grape grower.

My desire was simply to spend time with people whose lives revolved around biblical themes. I had a feeling that their experiences would jimmy the lock to unknown meaning and depth in Scripture. I got far more than I ever could've imagined.

Through conversations and interactions in warm living rooms and wet fields, I experienced Scripture in a way I never had before. My adventure further illuminated the rift between the world I live in and the ancient world Jesus spoke from. As if culture and time weren't significant enough disconnects, people in the Bible lived in agrarian societies. When the prophets—including Jesus—spoke of sheep and shepherds, bees and honey, fields and harvests, grapes and vines, listeners understood their references in ways that I simply don't.

How can I truly understand what Jesus meant when He described Himself as the Good Shepherd or the Lamb of God when the only places I've encountered sheep are at caged petting zoos and presented medium-well on a plate at fancy restaurants? How can I comprehend the meaning of the promised land as a place overflowing with milk and honey when I normally buy the sugary sweetness in a plastic, bear-shaped container at my local grocery store? How can I grasp the urgency of Jesus' declaration that the fields are ripe for harvest when I've never lived on a farm? And how can I embrace the fullness of what it means to abide in Him when I buy my grapes at Costco?

With such a natural disconnect, it's no wonder that spending time with these men and women in their fields and barns taking in the sights, sounds, and smells allowed me to experience Scripture in unprecedented ways. It has jump-started a desire for deeper study and reminded me once again that Scripture truly is alive.

This Bible study is part story, part adventure, and part conversation. I hope this ensures you won't read portions of Scripture the same way again. This six-session experience contains postcards of the larger journey I went on in the book *Scouting the Divine*. If you enjoy this study, I hope you'll consider using the book as an accompaniment for your own journey. My hope and prayer for you is that through our upcoming time together you'll begin Scouting the Divine and go on your own adventure of getting to know the story of God like you never have before. And that you, too, will share what you're learning with others.

SESSION 1

WITH THE SHEPHERDESS

Encountering God as the Good Shepherd

Like stinky cheese and fine wine, some ideas just get better with time. Though it's been nearly a decade since I first met Lynne, I'm still haunted by our chance conversation. I was in Sitka, Alaska, tending my aunt's bed and breakfast while she took a much-needed respite. Countless loads of laundry and dishes tried to temper my romantic notions of life at a three-bedroom inn. Nevertheless, I set the alarm extra early to pick fresh berries for rainbow-colored Alaskan scones designed to make Rachael Ray proud should she ever choose to visit.

The morning conversations with guests varied widely, but after only a few weeks they steadily became rote. Most of the dialogue involved answering questions about life in Alaska, places to shop, and the best hidden trails.

My initial conversation with Lynne followed this pattern. She and her husband, Tom, were on their inaugural trip to Alaska, one they dreamed about for years. In between bites of scone, I randomly asked what Lynne did with her free time.

"I'm a shepherdess," she said.

"Uh . . . what?" I asked quizzically.

"I have more than a dozen Shetland sheep that I breed and take care of," she said.

If you ever want to visit Alaska, taking a cruise is a great way to see much of the beauty the state offers. May is one of the best months to travel since it tends to rain less in late spring.

Shetland sheep originated in the Shetland Isles. As one of the smallest breeds, they are known for their fine and soft wool. They have no wool on their face, nose, legs, or ears. Each shade and pattern of wool has its own name based off of the original Shetland dialect. The rams can be 90 to 125 pounds, whereas the ewes may weigh between 75 and 100 pounds.

Sheep are the most frequently mentioned animal in the Bible.

Lynne explained that they had an open space behind their home where the sheep grazed and a barn to keep them safe at night. Intrigued by her passion for these woolly creatures, I couldn't hold back one particular question.

"Do you ever read the Bible?" I asked.

"I've read it before," she said suspiciously.

"I recently read John 10 where Jesus talks about being the Good Shepherd," I said, secretly hoping I wasn't sounding like one of *those* people. "Is it really true that sheep know their shepherd's voice?"

Lynne began sharing tales from her shepherding experience, drawing rich parallels between shepherding and God. I found myself hanging on her every word, but before we knew it she had to leave to catch a flight. On her way out the door, she offered to send me a collection of writings on sheep from a spiritual perspective.

I secretly hoped she wouldn't forget.

Three weeks later a manila file of articles arrived in the mail. As I read through the collection, I experienced a series of "Aha!" moments. If the truths of Scripture are like diamonds, then they were shifting ever so slightly to reveal a more captivating brilliance. I began understanding the biblical references to shepherding in a new light.

Have you ever met anyone who because of their experience or profession helped illuminate a portion of Scripture for you?

When was the last time you were around someone who made you hungry to know God and His Word even more? What about that person drew you to God?

On a scale of 1 to 10, how hungry are you to know God and His Word right now? What steps can you take to stir up the hunger in your own heart to know God and His Word even more?

RECONNECTING WITH THE SHEPHERDESS

Nearly 10 years have passed since that fateful morning with Lynne. I ended up moving to the great white north and marrying an extra-tall Alaskan. Then I moved again—this time to my home state of Colorado with my husband, Leif—and I stumbled upon the shepherdess' gift tucked deep in a file drawer of miscellaneous articles and memorabilia. As I flipped through the writings, the familiar hunger swelled inside of me. I wanted to experience shepherding firsthand. I wanted to live the story, celebrate the insights, and once again become captivated by our breathtakingly beautiful God.

I needed to track down Lynne. Where was she living? Was she still a shepherdess? Would she remember me? I googled Lynne's name and the word "sheep" and was delighted to discover a series of articles about Lynne and her farm—one of which listed her contact information. Getting the information was easy, but how do you go about reconnecting with someone you met once and haven't seen for years? Understanding that this wasn't the norm, I sent two e-mails in an attempt to warmly reintroduce myself and jog her memory of our initial encounter. They went without reply. I bravely picked up the phone.

Without an answer after three rings, I left a voicemail message that felt disjointed, a humble attempt to refresh her memory of their stay in my aunt's bed and breakfast years before. I expressed an interest in her shepherding, hoping I didn't sound strange, or worse, like some kind of wool-stalker. Hanging up, I spoke a soft prayer.

Lynne called later that afternoon. Upon hearing her voice, I felt a rush of relief. While she clearly remembered her Alaskan adventures, Lynne only vaguely remembered our encounter, and she never received my e-mails. I gently reminded her of our discussion and the articles she mailed.

"Is there any way I could spend an afternoon with you and the sheep?" I asked, unsure if I crossed the line into forced hospitality.

Watch the teaching segment "Encountering God as the Good Shepherd" from the *Scouting the Divine* DVD to see Margaret expand even more on just how good our Good Shepherd is. You can watch the video during your *Scouting the Divine* study group or download it for yourself at margaretfeinberg.com.

While taking care of her aunt's bed and breakfast, Margaret met her future husband, Leif, who was born and raised in Sitka, Alaska. He's 6'8" tall. She's only 5'6".

Start your own *Scouting the Divine* study group on Facebook. Invite your friends to join. Share observations and comments about your experience as you dig into the study.

"I think we could make that happen," she offered.

Over the next few weeks, we determined that the weekend after Memorial Day would be our best chance for good weather. Lynne and Tom graciously extended their invitation to include dinner and an overnight stay in their home. We agreed to bring juicy steaks and gourmet chocolates for dessert. I beamed at the beautiful irony of life: The two people I served at a bed and breakfast years earlier now opened their home to us.

SHEEP THROUGHOUT SCRIPTURE

Before packing for my trip to spend time with Lynne, I spent a great deal of time diving into Scripture to grasp the Bible's perspective on these woolly creatures—and it had a lot to say! With nearly 700 references to sheep and shepherds, ewes and lambs, and the various predators they face, I was taken back by how often sheep are mentioned in the Bible.

Have you ever considered how many different places sheep are mentioned in Scripture? Why do you think these animals are so prominent in the Bible?

What are your favorite Scriptures that mention sheep?

Why do you think the Bible often compares people to sheep instead of some other kind of animal?

® For an insightful book about the biblical emphasis on shepherding, consider reading *A Shepherd Looks at Psalm 23* by Phillip Keller.

® Be sure to check out the *Scouting the Divine* book that accompanies this Bible study. Through your reading, you'll not only learn more about Margaret's travels, you'll discover more insights into Scripture, too.

From the beginning, sheep line the pages of Genesis. Though sheep are not specifically mentioned in the account of creation, God made these animals as a source of food and clothing. Because of their value, they often became the center of contention and strife. The original bloody conflict between Cain and Abel was over an offering—the acceptable gift from the flock versus a rejected gift of the field (Genesis 4:2-5). The split between Lot and Abram was also sheep-related as the duo discovered the land wouldn't sustain their flocks (Genesis 13:4-6). And Abram's son, Isaac, made the Philistines jealous with his abundant flocks (Genesis 26:14).

But sheep were also used to garner goodwill. When Pharaoh wanted to win favor with Abram, he gave him sheep among other gifts (Genesis 12:14-16). Abram's grandson, Jacob, fell head over heels in love with a shepherdess named Rachel. Their initial love connection was at a well while watering sheep (Genesis 29:9-11). Though Jacob was a rascal, he eventually became who he was created to become: Israel. Toward the end of his life when he blessed his sons, he called on "the God who has been my shepherd all my life to this day" (Genesis 48:15-16). Though wild and rebellious in nature, something about his time in the fields with the flock made him acknowledge God as Shepherd.

Interestingly, Joseph also pastured the flocks. While on his way to see his brothers in the fields, he was waylaid by them and thrown into a pit (Genesis 37:12-24). Yet the prophetic dream of ruling over his brothers still came true. When Joseph was reunited with his family years later, it was his knowledge of shepherding that saved them. Joseph carefully instructed his brothers what to tell Pharaoh regarding the livestock. The information secured their position and provision in the land of Goshen, because every shepherd was loathsome to the Egyptians (Genesis 46:33-34).

Shortly after the story of the exodus began, Moses was on the run after his anger over an injustice got the best of him. Settling in the land of Midian, he saw another injustice: the daughters of the local priest struggling to water their flocks because of pushy shepherds. Moses helped them and was taken in by the family, marrying one of the daughters and becoming the very thing the Egyptians despised: a shepherd (Exodus 2:15-22). In fact, it was while Moses was pasturing a flock that God appeared to him as a blazing fire in the midst of a bush and called him to set the Israelites free (Exodus 3:1-3,10). Through a wild series of miracles, Pharaoh finally granted Moses' demand. God's people were set free but not without their flocks or herds.

Abel sacrificed the firstborn of his flock. It can be inferred from the text that Cain's offering was not of the first fruits of his crop. Read the full story in Genesis 4:2-8.

The land of Canaan had few water sources and limited grazing regions, so it's no wonder Abram and Lot outgrew the region. Lot took his flock east, into the plains of the Jordan—near Sodom and Gomorrah. Abram stayed in Canaan with his flock. To read about their split, visit Genesis 13:2-18.

The Midianites were descendants of Abraham through his wife Keturah, the same people who bought Joseph from his brothers and sold him into slavery. These were a nomadic people who lived in the desert. It was unusual for the Midianites to extend hospitality to Moses, a Jew, since the Midianites were a people hostile to Israel.

The books of the Law, presumably written by Moses, are filled with rules regarding livestock, particularly in regard to offerings, and the final book of the Torah informs readers what to do if they see a neighbor's sheep straying. (Bring it back, of course!)

Read Deuteronomy 22:1. How is obeying this command a fulfillment of Luke 10:27 and Deuteronomy 6:5?

Though he was far from perfect, King David had an incredible love and appreciation for the laws and commandments of God. A great example of this is Psalm 119. This psalm is an acrostic poem; each stanza begins with successive letters of the Hebrew alphabet, and the verses of each stanza begin with that same letter.

King David, described as "a man after God's own heart," spent years on rocky hillsides caring for sheep. His life story as well as the Psalms abound with references to shepherding and sheep (Psalms 78, 79, 100, 119). This is the man who inspired the words:

"Come, let us worship and bow down, let us kneel before the Lord our Maker. For He is our God, and we are the people of His pasture and the sheep of His hand" (Psalm 95:6-7).

Job's grand loss and even grander restoration involved sheep. Job lost (almost) everything. When the Lord chose to bless Job again, He doubled his portion to include 14,000 sheep—twice as many as before his testing (Job 1:3,16; 42:12).

In the DVD teaching for this session, you'll notice Margaret is wearing a red jacket. This is meant to subtly symbolize the sacrifice of sheep and the death of Jesus for the forgiveness of sins.

In the wise King Solomon's wooing of the Shulammite woman, he referred to her teeth as "a flock of ewes" (Song of Songs 6:6), a sheepish way of admiring her ivory smile. Isaiah wrote that in heaven we will find lambs resting alongside wolves in the age to come (Isaiah 11:6). The prophet painted a rich portrait of God as a tender shepherd caring for His people (Isaiah 40:10-12). Indeed, many of the prophets including Hosea (Hosea 4:16), Jeremiah (Jeremiah 3:14-16), Ezekiel (Ezekiel 34), Micah (Micah 2:12-13), Nahum (Nahum 3:18), and Zechariah (Zechariah 10:3) used shepherd imagery. Even Amos, one of the quirkiest guys in the Bible, was a shepherd turned prophet (Amos 1:1).

Maybe the most compelling use for sheep in the Old Testament, however, centers on their use as sacrifices. In that time, the sheep was the animal God chose to be symbolic of His deliverance and redemption. The animal pointed toward salvation. On their way out of slavery, the Israelites shared an unforgettable meal: the Passover lamb. Smearing the blood of lambs on the doorways of their houses caused the plague of death to "pass over" them.

Even before the exodus, in that unforgettable moment when Abraham raised his knife on his own son, he looked behind him to discover a ram caught by the horns in a nearby thicket. The ram became a substitute offering and Abraham named the place "The LORD Will Provide" (Genesis 22:13-14).

Centuries later, God provided. Waiting for the Messiah, the people eagerly anticipated the one who would "shepherd My people Israel" (Matthew 2:6). The promised one was the Son of God.

With God's calling clearly displayed in so many shepherds' lives, it should be no wonder that shepherds were included at Jesus' birth (Luke 2:8-18). Upon seeing his cousin, John the Baptist declared, "Behold, the Lamb of God!" (John 1:32-36). Throughout His teaching, Jesus referred to shepherds and sheep regularly and painted vivid concepts the people understood. Paul and Peter referred to these animals and their tender care in their writings. Imprisoned on the island of Patmos, John continued mentioning the Lamb he kept seeing in his apocalyptic visions. From Genesis to Revelation, the presence—and importance—of sheep in the Bible is unmistakable.

THE DOOR OF THE SHEEP

After our arrival, Lynne and Tom graciously welcomed us into their home. We settled into the guest room, then Lynne invited me to go meet her flock. I jumped at the chance. I followed her out of the back of their house, through a barn, and up a muddy path. One of the first things I noticed was that Lynne carefully opened and closed each gate, double-checking they were secure.

"You always have to be careful with gates," Lynne said. "For the animals, it's crucial to their survival. Not only do they keep the animals in—they keep the predators out."

Lynne's words reminded me of something I had been reading about. In ancient times the flock had to be kept in a stone or wood area overnight and then led to a new field for grazing each day. Shepherds often slept across the openings of their homemade sheepfolds, guarding the animals from predators and thieves with their own

Passover, or Pesach, is still celebrated within Jewish communities today. One of the observances of this holiday is the removal of all leavened bread from the home. It serves as a reminder that the Jews who fled Egypt were in such a hurry that there was no time to let their bread rise. At a deeper level, leaven is symbolic of pride, arrogance, or "puffiness." Passover is a time to remember the humbling truth that God delivers His people not because of their goodness but because of His mercy and to get rid of the spiritual leaven in our lives.

To learn more about sacrificial offerings of sheep, including their wool, read section 1.12, "The Best," in *Scouting the Divine*.

bodies. When Jesus described Himself as "the gate [or door]" of the sheep in John 10:9, He was painting a rich portrait of being both protector and provider.

> In what ways have you experienced Jesus as your protector and provider?

Listen to "Shepherd" by Todd Agnew from the *Scouting the Divine* playlist. Your group leader can e-mail you the whole playlist, or you can download it at *margaretfeinberg.com*.

> Do you feel like Jesus usually has to keep you in or the predators out? Why?

> Have you ever experienced a time when, like the shepherds of ancient days, you felt God was protecting you from harm? If so, explain.

"The utility of the law is, that it convinces man of his weakness, and compels him to apply for the medicine of grace, which is in Christ."[1]
—Augustine of Hippo

THE HIDDEN GIFT OF BOUNDARIES

Though rules and regulations can be aggravating, boundaries are essential to a sheep's survival—and our own. From a sheep's perspective, the fences only prevent them from enjoying greener grass; from a shepherd's perspective, the fences ensure their protection, provision, and a long, good life. This is particularly true of the Ten Commandments. When Moses traveled up Mount Sinai, God gave him 10 specific directives or boundaries for the people.

> Read Exodus 20:1-17. When you read the Ten Commandments, do you tend to view them from a sheep's perspective—the commandments only prevent you from enjoying greener grass—or from a shepherd's perspective—the fences ensure your protection, provision, and a long, good life? Why?

Which perspective—the sheep's or the shepherd's—makes you want to obey God's commands more? Why do you think perspective is so important when it comes to walking in obedience to God?

In the following chart, fill in how each of God's commandments helps protect, provide, and ensure a long life for you.

No.	Commandment:	Reward of Obedience:
1	No other gods	Example: Obeying this command helps us not get distracted by false gods with false promises who will only disappoint, hurt, and fail to save. Remaining true to God is a proper response to God's promise to remain true to us and never leave or forsake us.
2	No idols	
3	Don't take the Lord's name in vain	
4	Remember the Sabbath Day	
5	Honor your father and your mother	

At first glance, the First and Second Commandments seem to teach the same thing—a prohibition of idols. But during the Reformation, a popular interpretation of the Second Commandment involved physical images of God, like religious pictures and statues. Consequently, many Reformation-era churches removed all art.

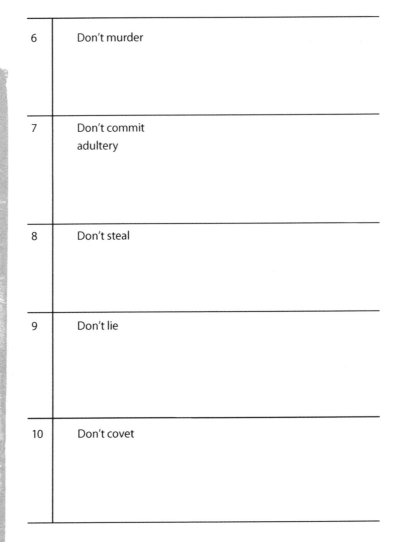

6	Don't murder
7	Don't commit adultery
8	Don't steal
9	Don't lie
10	Don't covet

The Ten Commandments starring Charlton Heston remains one of the greatest motion pictures of all time. This 1956 production was nominated for seven Academy Awards and is still shown on TV in conjunction with Easter.

How often do you think about the "why" behind God's commands? Why is that?

Listen to the audio segment called "Meet Lynne the Shepherdess" this week. Your group leader will send it to you via e-mail, or you can download it at margaretfeinberg. com. These audio recordings are designed to help you connect more deeply with the Good Shepherd as you spend time Scouting the Divine.

Does reflecting on the rewards and promises of obeying God give you a greater appreciation for the boundaries He establishes for you? Why or why not?

+

Margaret would love to see a picture from your study group. So this week, take a picture and send it to her at *hello@margaretfeinberg.com*. Then check back to see your photo posted on her site.

THE VOICE OF THE SHEPHERDESS

As we crested the hill, Lynne tugged the final gate closed and we looked out on the upper field. Sheep dotted the grassy expanses. Those closest to us stared at us—their mouths rhythmically moving—chewing fresh grass. Those in the distance remained undisturbed. "As soon as they hear my voice, they'll come running," Lynne whispered to ensure the sheep couldn't hear her.

Lynne was simply stating a fact that she knew to be true. She was a shepherdess. These were her sheep. For her, the statement was just cause and effect. For me, the statement was a defining moment in my spiritual adventure. Were the words of Jesus—the promise that like sheep we will hear and recognize His voice—really true? I felt a lump swell in my throat.

"Sheep, sheep, sheep," Lynne said.

At the sound of the first syllable, the flock bolted toward her. The sheep were responding to the voice of their shepherd.

The scene confirmed what Jesus described in John 10. This particular passage comes at an intriguing time. In the previous chapter, we read that Jesus performed an amazing miracle—He healed a man born blind. This one act set off a storm of controversy, in part because Jesus chose to heal the man on the Sabbath. The Pharisees, ever the sticklers for rules, had such a hard time with this man's healing that they interrogated him about what had happened. Unable to accept his responses or his healing, they excommunicated him. Yet Jesus found the man and affirmed to him that He was the Son of God. The man's response was simply, "Lord, I believe" (John 9:38).

The healing of the blind man wasn't the only time when Jesus brought up the issue of sheep and shepherding in the context of healing on the Sabbath. Consider Matthew 12:9-14. The Pharisees were supposed to be the shepherds of the sheep of Israel, and yet they proved themselves to be untrustworthy. Perhaps that's why Jesus kept using the imagery of shepherding when speaking to the religious leaders.

After the healing and transformation of the blind man, Jesus addressed the issue of spiritual blindness. The Pharisees were the first to speak up and ask, "We are not blind too, are we?" (John 9:40).

Interestingly, at this point Jesus shifted the topic from spiritual blindness to the importance of spiritual hearing and listening to the voice of God.

> **Read John 9:41–10:5 *aloud*. How do you recognize the voice of God in your own life?**

R

Read more about hearing and discerning God's voice in another resource from Margaret Feinberg called *The Sacred Echo: Hearing God's Voice in Every Area of Your Life.*

> **How do you discern that the voice you're hearing is truly from God and not from a stranger? What are some of the distinctive characteristics of the voice of God?**

During the filming of the first DVD teaching segment, the llamas and sheep kept eating the hay on the set. The producers had to push the sheep away several times to preserve the set.

Time and trust. That was why Lynne's sheep recognized her. It was because she was willing to put in the hard work of developing a relationship with them—even when they might not have wanted one with her. Throughout their lives, she was there. She called to them, cared for them, and acted in their best interest. And now? They knew her voice. But even more than knowing her voice, they knew she could be trusted. I couldn't help but wonder, *Do I feel the same way about Jesus?*

THE MISSING SHEEP

The sheep followed the muddy path down the trail. Lynne stood still and alert, never allowing her eyes to wander from the sheep. "I'm always counting because you never know when one will remain in the field from sickness or injury," she said.

You and Jesus both, I thought.

Jesus knew what it was like to search for a missing sheep. He even told a parable illustrating this idea. In Luke 15, Jesus described a shepherd who had a hundred sheep and lost one of them. He left the 99 to search for the lost sheep, and when he found it, he placed it on his shoulders and carried it home. Then he gathered all of his friends and neighbors together and retold the story in celebration. Jesus compared the rejoicing in the community to the rejoicing in heaven when one person who is away from God repents and returns to a vibrant relationship with Him.

In ancient Israel, a flock of a hundred sheep represented a great deal of wealth. Some Bible scholars believe that many sheep may have represented the collective animals of an entire community. It's unlikely that the shepherd was working alone; he probably had a few assistants alongside him. When the sheep disappeared, he didn't abandon the rest of the flock. That would've been foolish. Instead he left them in the care of one of the flock's other overseers.

Now there's a good chance that the news of the lost sheep would've quickly become a village concern. If this was the community's flock, then the entire community was waiting for the shepherd's return.

Meanwhile the shepherd searched for the lost animal. He hiked up steep hills and into dark ravines. When he found the sheep, he placed the 50-plus pound animal on his back and began the long journey home—no small feat when navigating tough terrain.

When he returned home, he announced the good news to his friends and neighbors. Without access to television or modern entertainment, the shepherd's story was probably the talk of the town. People wanted to hear every juicy detail. He probably told the story countless times.

Though I had read the story from Luke 15 many times before, I never realized until watching Lynne that shepherds carefully keep track of their flocks by constantly counting. That's how the shepherd in the parable knew a sheep was missing. He was carefully watching and counting. When he discovered that one of the sheep was gone, he set out to bring it back.

In the silence, I found myself with a new appreciation for God's faithfulness and goodness. Second Chronicles 16:9 describes the eyes of the Lord moving "to and fro throughout the earth" looking to strongly support those whose hearts are completely His. Maybe that's why Jesus said, "Are not five sparrows sold for two cents? Yet not one

Luke 15 is sometimes called "The Lost Parables" since it contains three of Jesus' stories about things that were lost and found: the sheep, a coin, and a son. In each instance, the one seeking throws a lavish celebration when what was lost is found.

"When I consider Your heavens, the work of Your fingers, the moon and the stars, which You have ordained; what is man that You take thought of him, and the son of man that You care for him? Yet You have made him a little lower than God, and You crown him with glory and majesty!" (Psalm 8:3-5).

of them is forgotten before God," and declared, "The very hairs of your head are all numbered" (Luke 12:6-7). God carefully watches everything; He is always scanning—noticing the tiniest details. Indeed, we don't serve a God who is far off, but One who is near and more involved in leading, guiding, and protecting us than we realize.

Read Luke 15:4-6 *aloud*. After arriving home safely with the sheep, what's the first thing the shepherd does?

Why is community—in both the high and low moments—so important to our spiritual journeys?

Jesus drew a comparison between the celebration of the shepherd and the celebration of God when one person repents and changes his or her life. How does the shepherd imagery of the parable illustrate this point?

For a funny video clip of what some shepherds in Wales tried with their sheep, search for the "Extreme Sheep LED Art" post on *youtube.com*.

To read about Lynne's first encounter holding a baby ewe named Swan, read section 1.10, "A Shepherd's Embrace," in *Scouting the Divine*.

THE GOOD SHEPHERD

God isn't just a shepherd—He's a *good* shepherd. A good shepherd is willing to risk himself as the door of the sheep to protect them. A good shepherd carefully watches over and keeps count of the sheep to make sure they are all safe. A good shepherd always watches the gates to make sure the sheep are protected and don't wander into harm's way. A good shepherd knows his sheep and the sheep know their shepherd. The sheep respond to the shepherd's voice. And a good shepherd is willing to take great risks to go after a single lost sheep.

How "good" of a shepherd do you really think God is?

What experiences have you had that have shaped your beliefs? Are there any areas in which you're struggling to trust God as the Good Shepherd?

Why is knowing God as the Good Shepherd so important? How will you respond to God if you think He is a bad shepherd?

Jesus made several "I am" statements in the Book of John, the most controversial coming in John 8. In that chapter, Jesus claimed that before the days of Abraham, "I am" (v. 58). The Jews interpreted this as blasphemy, since Jesus was applying the sacred name of God as revealed in Exodus 3 to Himself. In Exodus 3, God said His name was *Yahweh*, roughly translated as "I Am."

Watching Lynne interact with her sheep—the way she called them by name, fed them, and cared for their needs—revealed that she was a good and loving shepherd. But I couldn't help but wonder how she would respond to Jesus describing Himself as the Good Shepherd. Consider John 10:11-15:

"I am the good shepherd; the good shepherd lays down His life for the sheep. He who is a hired hand, and not a shepherd, who is not the owner of the sheep, sees the wolf coming, and leaves the sheep and flees, and the wolf snatches them and scatters them. He flees because he is a hired hand and is not concerned about the sheep. I am the good shepherd, and I know My own and My own know Me, even as the Father knows Me and I know the Father; and I lay down My life for the sheep."

"What do you think of this?" I asked.

In John 10, Jesus made the distinction of a "hireling" and the owner of the sheep. The hireling is a paid hand. The difference in the two would be seen when danger comes. The hireling would run, reasoning that it's just a job and not worth dying for. The owner would stay and fight for what are his.

"I think it's a great picture of being a shepherd," Lynne said. "It's all true. He who enters by the door is indeed the shepherd. He calls his sheep by name. He leads them out. He goes before them and the sheep follow. If a stranger came and opened my gate the sheep would run away. They really would flee. This is all a great metaphor."

Yet when Jesus spoke these words in John 10, they weren't just a great metaphor, but a tangible portrait of our God. A God who loves us more than we can know. A God who watches over us more than we can imagine. A God who cares for our individual needs more than we can hope. Indeed, Jesus is the Good Shepherd.

Later on in John 10, Jesus compared His followers to sheep and made a bold declaration. Look up John 10:27-28 and read it aloud. But let's not stop there—try re-reading verse 28 and inserting your own name in each blank:

> I give eternal life to (insert your name) _____,
> and (insert your name) _____ will never perish;
> and no one will snatch (insert your name) _____
> out of My hand.

Remember the children's movie, *Babe*? The little pig learns to be a good shepherd with the help of his sheep and dog friends. He learns to shepherd not by demands or rude language, but instead by guiding the sheep with kindness and love.

Spend a few moments meditating on the Scripture above. Do you really think Jesus' promise is true? Why or why not?

Can you think of someone else who would enjoy being part of your *Scouting the Divine* study? Why not invite them to join your Bible study group next week?

Is there anything holding you back from fully trusting Jesus' promise? Explain.

EMBRACING THE GOD-INFUSED LIFE

Knowing God as the Good Shepherd forces me to come to terms with my defenselessness and recognize just how much I need Him. It means knowing and trusting in His provision in every area of my life. At times, as the psalmist reflects in Psalm 23, God forcibly makes me lie down in green pastures, which is important because I have a natural propensity to skip the good things—including rest—He provides. Gently, He leads me beside quiet waters—special places where His spirit hovers, refreshing my own. In the stillness I become more attuned to His voice, myself, and all those around me. In this place, He restores my soul from the wear and tear—the weary and the teary—of everyday life.

In honor of His name, the Good Shepherd guides me in the paths of righteousness—the trails God has established rather than the ones I try to forge myself. Though there will be times I'll walk through some scary valleys, I'm not afraid because I know my Shepherd and my Shepherd knows me. He is near. His eyes are always scanning, I will not be picked off by predator or pestilence. Sometimes His rod disciplines me, other times His staff saves me. Though different from my own ways, I find comfort in His.

Though wolves and coyotes howl in the distance, I know when I'm close to my Shepherd I can safely enjoy the bounty of the field. In tenderness, my Shepherd even anoints my head with oil so the flies don't bug me, and my cup, the provision of the Shepherd's hand, overflows. As long as I am with my Shepherd, goodness and lovingkindness will accompany me every day, and I will dwell in the house of my God forever.

Apart from a healthy understanding of God as the Good Shepherd, I can never walk in the fullness of all He has called and created me to be. None of us can.

"When you can't sleep, don't count sheep. Talk to the Shepherd."
—Unknown

Make sure you have the contact information of everyone in your Bible study group so you can get in touch with them. This week, go online and tweet one thing you've learned through this session.

Lord, I want to know You as the Good Shepherd. Like a sheep, I'm completely and utterly dependent on You, the Good Shepherd, for everything. I ask You to remove the doubts and fears I have about following wherever You want to lead. Holy Spirit, reveal the distorted beliefs or misconceptions I have about You that lead me to believe You aren't really the Good Shepherd. Give me a fresh and clear picture of who You are through Scripture. Captivate me once again with Your love. In Jesus' name, amen.

ACTIVITY

Spend some time prayerfully meditating on Psalm 23. On a blank sheet of paper, rewrite the psalm as a personal prayer to God. Ask God to lead you, guide you, and protect you. It's a prayer God won't refuse!

SCRIPTURE MEMORY

"I am the good shepherd, and I know My own and My own know Me, even as the Father knows Me and I know the Father; and I lay down My life for the sheep" (John 10:14-15).

SCOUTING THE DIVINE

As you go through the upcoming week, pay attention to the things you encounter in everyday life and reflect on themes in the Bible. You may drive by a farm and think about the various agricultural themes in Scripture. Or you may pass by your county or state's government buildings and consider the widely varying political climates in Scripture. You may be spending time with kids and think about children who are mentioned in the Bible. Spend some time in Scripture studying your own theme—go ahead and scout the Divine.

SESSION
2

IN THE FIELDS

Reaching Out to the Marginalized

Following the trail back down to the lower field, Lynne began describing the characteristics of specific sheep.

"That's Opal," she said, pointing to a silver ewe. "She's a great mother, though this year she's more possessive of her lamb. Maybe it's because she gave birth to only one instead of two babies, and she lambed later than the rest. She has a weight problem. During her pregnancy, she was so large I honestly thought she was going to have triplets. Her voice is different from any of the others—it's raspy, more of a bleat than a baa-aa.

"This is Iris and her nickname is 'Herself,'" Lynne added, scratching one of the sheep under the chin. "She is self-confident and goes her own way. If there's an open door, she's the first to be out of it. Iris sure knows how to get into trouble, but on a warm, sunny day, she's also the first to come down and lie beside me."

Psalm 139 is noted for its extravagance and elegance. King David wrote this psalm intending to describe the wonders of God relating to His people.

I pointed to a sheep that looked older than the rest; its dark wool was uneven in length, its face scarred. "The black one, well, that's Meggie," Lynne explained. "She's 14—already two years beyond the average life expectancy—and as a granny she'll stomp her foot if she gets mad at you. But make no mistake; she's loving and kind."

One sheep seemed particularly taken with Lynne. She pushed against Lynne's leg in an effort to get additional attention. "That's Jovita; she's just the sweetest. She likes to sit on my lap, and she'll even nibble on my nose. I call her my 'lap sheep.' Dove, who had a difficult pregnancy, abandoned her, but Iris adopted her. Love that Iris. There's a lot of flock drama, you know."

I didn't know, but I was quickly learning. Sheep and people share more in common than I ever imagined. As we walked, Lynne described the sheep with the same tenderness of a mother describing her children, naming each one and telling all about them. Where I saw a flock of sheep, she saw individual animals with unique characteristics and quirks that made them even more endearing. I wondered if God sometimes sees us the same way.

> Read Psalm 139:13-16. Lynne knows her sheep intimately—their personalities, likes, and dislikes, as well as the inner-workings of their relationships. What parallels do you see between the way Lynne knows her sheep and the way God knows us?

What are some of the differences between the way Lynne knows her sheep and the way God knows us?

Reflecting on Psalm 139:13-16, how does it make you feel that God knows you so well? Does it bring comfort? Make you uncomfortable? A little bit of both? Explain.

How does knowing that God knows and loves you wholly change the way you see yourself? How does this change the way you see other people?

Is this truth motivational for you? In what sense?

Watch the teaching segment called "Reaching Out to the Marginalized" from the *Scouting the Divine* DVD to see Margaret discuss reaching out to the marginalized. You can watch the video during your *Scouting the Divine* study group or download it for yourself at margaretfeinberg.com.

A SHEPHERD'S HEART FOR A SICK SHEEP

"Through there," Lynne instructed, closing the gate behind us.

I took a few steps forward and then I saw her: Piaget. Even if she hadn't been sporting a diaper-like wrap fashioned from an old T-shirt, I knew this sheep wasn't well. I walked slowly toward her, softly saying her name. She looked at me hesitantly and moved swiftly away. Though in a penned area, she managed to stay equidistant away from me no matter which way I turned. I finally realized the most gracious and humane thing for me to do with this sick, skittish creature was to stand still.

"Piaget."

When Lynne spoke her name, the sheep instantly perked up her head and walked expectantly toward her. Without question, Piaget knew her shepherdess's voice.

Piaget was named after Jean Piaget, a 20th-century Swiss psychologist who is well known for his study of children. His theory, the stages of cognitive development, is still taught today.

Though varied in size, sheep have good hearing and are sensitive to noise when being handled. They also possess excellent peripheral vision and can see behind themselves without turning their heads.

Sheep have distinct economic advantages when compared with other livestock. They don't require expensive housing like chickens or pigs, and they are an efficient use of land; roughly six sheep can be kept on the amount of land that would suffice for a single cow or horse.

Lynne kneeled on the ground gently scratching the ewe under the chin. "Come on over now," she invited me.

Unhurried yet deliberate, I moved forward. This time Piaget didn't move. In the presence of her shepherdess, Piaget knew she was safe. I knelt down beside Lynne. She taught me how to place my hand palm up and wiggle my fingers in a sort of beckoning motion. Piaget moved her chin from Lynne's hand to my own, and I felt the exhilaration of connecting with a sheep I had only read about.

Lynne e-mailed me several weeks before our arrival to inform me that one of her most precious sheep, Piaget, was sick. One evening in early May, Lynne noticed that Piaget was the last to come down from the upper pasture. The young ewe had recently given birth to twins, Miguel and Mario, who immediately took to their mother. Concerned by her slow gait, Lynne watched Piaget extra closely to make sure she was eating properly.

When Lynne called the sheep from the upper pasture the next afternoon, Piaget was nowhere to be found. Lynne discovered the ewe resting in the middle of the field alone. Upon seeing Lynne and hearing her voice, Piaget slowly got up and walked toward the shepherdess.

Lynne knew something was seriously wrong. Her temperature was over 106—four dangerous degrees above normal. One side of Piaget's udder was hot and hard, and she had no interest in grain or her lambs. Lynne administered nutrients and vitamins and massaged her udder.

Recording the day's events in her journal, she decided to share the news with her fellow shepherds—those who would understand, those who would pray, those who would offer wisdom or insight. She didn't resist signing, "I love Piaget" before sending the first of what would be many e-mails to follow.

When Lynne returned home from work the next afternoon, she expected to see some improvement in Piaget. Instead, all she saw was a very sick sheep. Piaget wobbled as spasms deformed her weakening body, the involuntary jarring motions painful to watch. Lynne wondered how long Piaget could survive.

Lynne miraculously managed to find an on-call veterinarian who promised to be at the farm within 20 minutes, but she wondered if Piaget would last even that long. She prepared herself for the worst and waited.

The vet confirmed that Piaget was dangerously ill: An infection in her udder was wreaking havoc on her immune system and she was battling pneumonia. Most shepherds would put down a sheep that sick, but not Lynne. She loved her sheep.

Lynne sent the following message to her shepherding friends:

It's 11:15 p.m., and I just hooked up bag number six for Piaget. Each bag will last eight hours depending on the dripping schedule, but I do not think that Piaget will be here for another eight hours. I am so tired and have just spent the last hour or so with her. I sort of wanted to spend the night lying beside her, but my sense is that she was ready for some alone time. I lay with her for awhile and told her what a special ewe she is and that if she had to go that was OK. Along with me, she has tried so very hard to fight through this thing, but my sense is that it's getting the better of her.

Throughout the day Piaget gave me moments of hopefulness when she wanted to chew on straw or when she sucked down a few cups of electrolytes. There were times when she pawed my leg so that I would put my hands on her for a scratch. One time she had alert eyes and that very "Piaget-ish" head tilt. But tonight she is not too responsive and she is breathing so short and labored.

While Piaget is still sort of here, I have said good-bye. I need to crawl into bed, but I smell very much like a sheep. I guess that is not a new thing for Tom. Even though I know nothing will have changed much, I can't resist one more visit to Piaget. This time I will be quiet and not disturb her.

Reading Lynne's entry revealed just how intimate her relationship with Piaget had become. Afraid of what she would find the next morning, Lynne asked Tom to make the journey to the barn and report on his findings.

"She's still alive," he announced. To Lynne's delight Piaget exhibited interest in eating straw. Lynne carefully administered antibiotics and fluids before heading off to work, and did so again as soon as she returned home. Before tucking herself into bed, she wrote:

I am so far behind on my personal stuff. Tomorrow is my last Spanish class. I decided to go out and sit with [Piaget] to do my homework for tomorrow. I knew that perhaps we were over the hump when she tried to eat my Spanish book. I tried to take her on a walk today, but

Be intentional about building community in your Bible study group. Who is the person in your group you'd like to get to know better? Set up a time over the next week to go for a walk, grab coffee, or enjoy lunch together.

"If you have men who will exclude any of God's creatures from the shelter of compassion and pity, you will have men who will deal likewise with their fellow men."[3]
—St. Francis of Assisi

she was too weak to stand. She went a few steps and then sort of collapsed. I think tomorrow she will be a little stronger—but I'm not so sure about me. This has been one of the most trying sheep ordeals.

Lynne and Piaget

Something about the signature caught my attention. Lynne and Piaget—they were in this together. I wondered if the little sheep knew how much she was loved.

The next day Lynne's e-mail was full of hope. The spot on the udder looked worse, but Piaget was beginning to eat more—one of the crucial signs of a healthy sheep. At the end of the day, Lynne recorded:

I have two pretty full work days and I have cancelled all the unnecessary meetings so I do not have to be gone too long. This has been a really new experience. Previously I have either had a sick sheep that got better fast or who died fast—not one who has been this sick for days, but I am hopeful.

Tom says tonight that he is hopeful that if he ever gets this sick that he will be cared for in the same way.

When I was having my quiet time with Piaget tonight I realized that she is not a show sheep. She does not have many unique traits other than she is a Shetland. But tonight I realized that she and I have bonded over this time. She trusts me and I see in her a metaphor for how I wish the world was. So many people and creatures suffer and die needlessly that with just a little care could live out their potential. I think that one of the reasons we do what we do is that we can.

For me it's a special thing to be able to do this thing that some would think is silly, but the ability to do what we do in some small way lets us honor life. We cannot make life and sometimes we cannot save life, but we can use all the wisdom we have to make a difference in a life. I hope that I can make a difference for Piaget. Thanks for being my sheep family.

Lynne's message revealed a rich lesson about not just caring for sheep, but caring for each other. In good times and in bad, we need a community to help look after us, what Lynne called her sheep family: those we ask for help, wisdom, insight, hope, encouragement, and prayer. A sheep family celebrates new life but also mourns losses. A sheep family maintains a special connection that transcends differences and brings them together on occasions such as this.

President Woodrow Wilson grazed sheep on the south lawn of the White House. The wool was sold to raise money for the Red Cross during World War I.

"Trust the past to the mercy of God, the present to His love, and the future to His providence."
—Augustine of Hippo

Lynne knew she needed a family. We all do. Her community played an important role—encouraging her with phone calls, responding to her e-mails, and offering support.

Who is part of your community as you're going through life? Who do you call on when times get tough?

Why do you think it's important to be a part of a community?

Throughout the next few weeks, Lynne watched Piaget hang in the balance between life and death. During this time, she began to notice an unmistakable change in Piaget. Usually sheep hate being separated from the flock, but while she was sick, Piaget paid no attention to the sheep on the other side of the wall. She didn't call for them; instead she only called for her shepherdess. That evening Lynne wrote:

> I know that my sheep know me, but this was a different type of knowing—I really felt known. Along with this knowing was an awareness of the great trust that Piaget has developed for me over these weeks. I have a few other sheep that I am treating—one for a cloudy eye and another for a little cough. Neither sickness is serious, but each sheep fights the treatment. But it's not so with Piaget. She tolerates anything I do and seems to have a sense of peace about it all. As I experience her trust and her knowing me I just feel a warm joy.

As I read these words, I wondered if Lynne was writing about a relationship with sheep or a relationship with God. All too often in my own life I've seen myself fighting God's activity, afraid the direction He's steering me in or the preventative care He's prescribing isn't in my best interest. Yet I long for a relationship with God like that between Piaget and Lynne—not just where I tolerate what God wants to do but actually celebrate it with a sense of unmistakable peace and trust, knowing He truly is the Good Shepherd.

"There is only one thing more painful than learning from experience and that is not learning from experience."[5]
—Archibald MacLeish, poet and Pulitzer prize winner

It is estimated that one pound of wool can make 10 miles of yarn.

Sometimes getting involved in another's life is difficult, tiring, and expensive—like Lynne's care for Piaget, it can cost us more than we expect. Have you ever cared for or been there for someone else during a time of sickness, loss, or suffering? What was it like?

What was the most challenging aspect of your involvement? What did you learn through your involvement?

Lynne is a loving, kind, and good shepherd, but not all shepherds treat their sheep so well. To learn more, read section 1.15, "Bad Shepherd," in the *Scouting the Divine* book.

How did you grow personally and spiritually?

Re-read the e-mails Lynne sent to her sheep family and underline anything that catches your attention or surprises you. What parallels do you see between the tender care Lynne had for Piaget and the tender care God has for each of us?

THE REBELLIOUS RAM

I followed Lynne into the lower pasture where we both squatted on the ground. On her way through the barn, she scooped up some grain. With the cry, "Sheep, sheep, sheep," young rams and eager ewes were pressing up against her for a handful of sheep treats. The flock slowly warmed up to me, not because of anything I did or said, but because I was near their shepherdess.

I beckoned the sheep the way Lynne taught me. At first hesitant, the sheep slowly responded to the invitation, each taking its turn being scratched under the chin.

Upset that he wasn't the center of attention, one of the youthful rams, Alano, began ramming me with his horns. The first time was gentle and sweet, but the moment he stepped back to get a running start the winsomeness vanished.

"Lynne!" I cried out.

"You can't let him do that!" she said sternly. "Grab him by the horn."

I reached out, grabbed one of the horns, and held him at arm's length. "No!" I said firmly. Foolishly thinking Alano lost his machismo, I released him. He took a few steps back and rammed me again.

"He has to be disciplined now," she said, grabbing the rambunctious ram by one horn. Dragging Alano into another fenced section, Lynne sat him in isolation from the other sheep. She returned to the grass beside me, and together we watched as Alano stood at the gate wanting back in. His baa-aa's sounded more like moans. Alano was one unhappy ram. Lynne explained that if she didn't discipline Alano, he would grow up to be a dangerous ram and of no use to anyone.

Some shepherds use time-out, others have a squirt bottle on hand, and there are those who try more creative methods (including neutering), but in the end, if a ram grows up and has no fear of its shepherd and no respect for other sheep, the most humane act is to destroy it.

"If a ram does not fear me, then he will grow up and try to injure me and the other sheep. An uncontrollable ram can cause immense damage to a flock," Lynne explained. "Two rams like that will keep running toward each other until one, or on rare occasions both, die."

Watching Alano's self-inflicted misery sent a wave of gratitude through my heart for the discipline of God. Without it we not only lose respect for God but for others. The resulting damage is immeasurable. At times, the weight of the Spirit's conviction—what feels like the goring of my soul—seems too much to bear. But those instances, awful though they seem, are blessings in disguise (Hebrews 12:10-11). Alano was a portrait of this simple truth.

For the sheep that always wanders off—and leads other sheep astray in the process—a shepherd may resort to breaking a leg of the sheep. Then the shepherd would hand feed the sheep and carry it until the bone mended, hopefully curing it of its desire to wander.

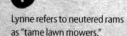

Lynne refers to neutered rams as "tame lawn mowers."

Read Hebrews 12:10-11. How do you usually respond to God's discipline? Do you easily submit or are you more like Alano?

In what ways is the discipline of God a sign of His love? How have you seen that in your own life?

"Without a shepherd sheep are not a flock."[6]
—Russian Proverb

How does knowing that God's discipline produces the "fruit of righteousness" (v. 11) affect your attitude toward such discipline?

Watching Alano's rebellious behavior made me wonder if Lynne had ever had a sheep that was impossible to deal with.

"One sheep we called 'The Brat.' Sometimes you have a sheep that is so smart it's always getting out, getting into trouble, and causing all kinds of problems," Lynne said. She explained that The Brat always watched the gates. The moment Lynne or Tom opened a gate, she would bolt to escape. The ewe didn't know what she wanted to do once she got out; she only knew she wanted to be free. She didn't realize the best possible life was inside the gate.

Have you ever known or worked with someone like The Brat? What kinds of challenges did that person create because of his or her rebellious nature?

What kinds of struggles and tensions are created if you're always looking for an open gate and an opportunity to escape?

Have you ever been The Brat? In what ways do you long to be free? Who are you looking to in order to experience freedom?

What do you think holds you back from experiencing contentment right where you are?

"Not that I speak from want, for I have learned to be content in whatever circumstances I am. I know how to get along with humble means, and I also know how to live in prosperity; in any and every circumstance I have learned the secret of being filled and going hungry, both of having abundance and suffering need. I can do all things through Him who strengthens me" (Philippians 4:11-13).

THE INCLUSION OF SHEPHERDS

We spent the afternoon in the fields among the sheep, only slipping inside briefly to grab a hot soup and sandwich lunch with Tom and Leif. There was something unmistakably peaceful about being with the flock, watching the slow but steady movement of their jaws as they chewed on grass, and feeling the warm sun on my cheeks.

As I studied the presence of sheep and shepherds throughout Scripture, I noticed that it was often the younger siblings who were responsible for shepherding, while older children were given more important roles. For example, even though Cain was older, Abel kept the flocks (Genesis 4:2). When Samuel was sent by God to anoint one of the sons of Jesse to be the future king of Israel, he fully expected one of the older sons to be the

Rachel and Leah's father, Laban, played a cruel trick on Jacob. He told Jacob he could marry Rachel if he spent seven years working for him. After seven years, Laban gave Jacob Leah instead. He had to work another seven years to marry Rachel. Read the whole story in Genesis 29.

one God chose. But it turned out to be the youngest son, David, who was anointed by Samuel. In order for Samuel to anoint David, David's father had to call him in from the fields where he was taking care of the sheep (1 Samuel 16:1-13).

Sometimes it wasn't the younger son, but the younger daughter. Rachel, a little sister to Leah, was recognized as a shepherdess in Genesis 29:2-11. While watering sheep at a well, Rachel met Jacob and fell in love.

Lynne confirmed that this principle of the younger and weaker members of the family caring for the flocks still holds true today. On a recent trip to Peru, she spent time with several families who kept flocks. In the remote area she visited, the children, women, and even the elderly were the ones caring for the sheep. They traveled with a small satchel of food, an extra layer of clothing, and a knife for protection. I tried to imagine a fifth grader or grandma defending the flock from predators, but struggled to wrap my mind around such an image. Yet these are the family members who are often responsible for the entire family's livelihood and food supply.

Which means there's a good chance that when God sent a host of angels to tell the shepherds of Jesus' birth, those angels were inviting children, women, and perhaps the elderly— alongside the kings and wise men—to one of the greatest moments in history. In His loving care, God made sure that those who were all too often marginalized and overlooked were included in the celebration of the birth of His Son.

What makes God's inclusion of shepherds in His Son's birth even more amazing is that He associated with them at all. Culturally, shepherds weren't always considered reputable, upstanding members of society. They were often the family members who couldn't do a more skilled job. Over the years, shepherds became viewed with contempt and distrust.

Because of spending so much time alone searching for pasture for their animals, they were sometimes seen as socially awkward and disconnected. Because of their propensity to move, many viewed shepherds as thieves willing to take what they could when they needed it to simply survive. The reputation of the shepherds was a bit sketchy.

Yet these are the very people God included at the birth of Jesus. That may not seem like a big deal, but how many people were issued invitations to Jesus' birth? And how many of them received an angelic visit—an entire host of angels—delivering the news?

Read Luke 2:1-20 *aloud*. How does the image of shepherds as children, women, and the elderly change the way you read this story?

Throughout church history, Christianity has often been called a religion for women and slaves. The description was meant to capture the attractiveness the gospel had to people on the fringes of society.

How do you think the shepherds responded to the visit of an angel and then an entire heavenly host? How do you think you would have responded?

Recognizing the nomadic nature of shepherds, how quickly do you think word spread about the birth of Jesus (vv. 17-18)?

Why do you think God chose to include shepherds in the announcement of His Son?

"The Lord is their strength, and He is a saving defense to His anointed. Save Your people and bless Your inheritance; be their shepherd also, and carry them forever." (Psalm 28:8-9)

What does this inclusion say about God's heart for the young, weak, and marginalized? Why should we be concerned with the young, weak, and marginalized?

God's choice to announce His Son's birth to the shepherds was intentional. For centuries He had linked Himself with people on the margins; who else would He choose to send a birth announcement to?

Take a look at the following Scriptures:
- **Psalm 80:1**
- **Hebrews 13:20**
- **1 Peter 2:24-25**
- **1 Peter 5:4**

Does it surprise you that God so closely identifies Himself with those who live on the margins of society? What does that indicate about His character?

Jesus was often criticized for His association with outcasts. Yet that association was pivotal to His ministry, as Jesus described in Luke 4:18-19: "The Spirit of the LORD is upon me, because He anointed me to preach the gospel to the poor. He has sent me to proclaim release to the captives, and recovery of sight to the blind, to set free those who are oppressed, to proclaim the favorable year of the LORD."

God didn't play it safe when it came to the names used to describe Himself. He could have selected any title or name, and we might expect Him to identify Himself with someone more "important" in society. Instead, He reached out to the young, the weak, the old, and the outcast by embracing the name Shepherd.

In what ways is God challenging you to reach out to the young, the weak, the old, and the outcast?

What steps can you take to begin defending the defenseless and speaking up for those who have no voice?

SHEPHERD—WITH AND FOR US

By the time I left Lynne, I felt well-rested and well-fed. My mind brimmed with the spiritual lessons I had learned as I began to recognize God as Shepherd. While the names for God, including King, Lord, Savior, and Redeemer, are etched into my mind, the idea of thinking of God as Shepherd is less familiar. Yet recognizing God as Shepherd challenges me to trust Him even more. As the Good Shepherd, God cares for me more than I can ever imagine.

He is with me in moments of sickness, weakness, pain, and loss. He is not a God who is far off, but who climbs in the pen with me to provide comfort, healing, and encouragement. At times, God will discipline me, but even His rebuke is in my best interest. Apart from His discipline I can't become all He has called and created me to be. And the very fact that God would associate Himself with shepherds is a reminder that His arms are wide open to us all. No one, absolutely no one, is beyond the redeeming and restoring power of God. Which means we need to keep our eyes open to the surprising ways He wants to work in all of us—even in the lives of those we least expect.

Lord, I am grateful that You came into this world and associated Yourself with the weak, humble, and marginalized. Thank You for pursuing me. Forgive me for the times when I rebel and try to run away from You. Forgive me for the times when I foolishly think that if I do things my way, my life will be better. I need You. Continue to reveal Yourself to me as the Good Shepherd. Give me a shepherd's heart like Yours so that I, too, may be willing to reach out to those on the margins of society. Let me be a vessel of Your love. In Jesus' name, amen.

"Perhaps the most blessed element in this asking and getting from God lies in the strengthening of faith which comes when a definite request has been granted. What is more helpful and inspiring than a ringing testimony of what God has done?"[7]
—Rosalind Goforth, missionary, wife, and mother

Go online and share something you learned through this week's session using #scoutingthedivine.

ACTIVITY

Visit a local farmer who has sheep. Brainstorm a list of questions before you go. Learn as much as you can.

SCRIPTURE MEMORY

"Now the God of peace, who brought up from the dead the great Shepherd of the sheep through the blood of the eternal covenant, even Jesus our Lord, equip you in every good thing to do His will, working in us that which is pleasing in His sight, through Jesus Christ, to whom be the glory forever and ever. Amen" (Hebrews 13:20-21).

SCOUTING THE DIVINE

During the upcoming week, pay attention to people who are on the margins. They may be people who are particularly young or old; they may be homeless or on the brink of losing everything; they may be the ones who are overlooked at work or in your community. Prayerfully consider how you might go out of your way to include them, encourage them, serve them, and honor them. Remember that God sent a host of angels to the lonely shepherds to announce the coming of His Son. Go ahead, scout the Divine, and look for opportunities to be an extension of God's love, grace, and mercy.

NOTES

SESSION
3

ON THE FARM

Recognizing That Everything Has Its Season

We first met Joe while living in Juneau, Alaska. Joe was part of a group of faith-filled college students who had traveled to the northernmost state for the summer to serve the local community and grow spiritually. On their first visit to our church, we decided to invite them over for lunch. They jumped at the opportunity for a hot meal, proving once again that when you're a college student, the only thing better than food is free food.

The lunch was the first of many we shared with those students. Throughout the summer we saw them many times attending church, hanging out downtown, and crowding around our dining room table enjoying second and third helpings. After lunch most of the students disappeared. Except Joe.

This Nebraska native sprawled out on our oversized chair as afternoon turned into evening, talking about anything and everything. Lunch leftovers became dinner. Our conversations circled around life, God, and relationships, with too many almost-pee-your-pants bursts of laughter to count.

After my adventures with the shepherdess, I wanted to talk to a farmer next. With so many references to fields and harvest lining the Old and New Testaments, I was convinced that a farmer would have rich insights. When I mentioned the idea to Leif, he suggested I call Joe.

As of 2008, the approximate population of the whole state of Nebraska was 1,783,432. The approximate population of New York City was 8,363,710.[8]

Laughing for only 10 minutes each day has been proven to lower blood pressure and decrease pain in arthritic people.

Tornado Alley is a region including Nebraska, Kansas, Oklahoma, South Dakota, northern Texas, and eastern Colorado. It is home to the most powerful storms in the U.S. A tornado's winds can top 250 miles per hour and clear-cut a path a mile wide and 50 miles long.

At the first hint that we might visit, Joe yelled with glee, "You're coming to Nebraska!"

Though I'm still not sure he fully understood why we were coming, Joe assured me that he and his uncle were happy to spend time talking about farming. Our trip was scheduled for the last week of August during the alfalfa harvest. We flew into Omaha and drove to Sioux City where met up with Joe.

Dressed in shorts, a T-shirt, blue flip-flops, and his backwards ball cap, Joe greeted us with a wide smile. He gave each of us bear hugs; his energy and enthusiasm for life was as contagious as ever. We spent the afternoon together and agreed to meet the next morning to visit his uncle Aaron's farm.

We set out the next morning for our tour of the farm. Joe pointed to an open metal storehouse with five silver silos on the side of the road. "We're here!" he said with a grin.

Stepping out of the car, I knew I had finally arrived—in the middle of nowhere. Besides the storehouse, silos, two colorful stock cars, a Hot Slots billboard, and a few pieces of rusty equipment, rows of corn filled the landscape in every direction.

Joe gave us a tour of the farm. He carefully explained the purpose of each piece of equipment in the barn-shaped warehouse and then took us around the back to look at the silos. He pointed to one with a roof mangled like a soda can, the result of tornado force winds.

Looking at the crunched roof, I wondered how many natural things, like weather, farmers are more aware of than I am. Surely that wouldn't be the only thing. Agrarian metaphors run a steady thread throughout the Bible, and I had no doubt there was a lot about this farm for me to learn.

Walking toward one of the silos that was still intact, Joe asked if I wanted to see the grain inside. Eyeing the steep narrow metal ladder on the side of the silo, I taunted, "You first!" Joe scurried up the side of the silo wearing only flip-flops, opened a metal door frame, and yelled down, "Empty." He opened a lower door and we peeked inside—only a handful of dried corn stippled the dusty floor.

Looking inside the empty silo, I couldn't help but think about a farming parable Jesus told. A man had approached Jesus over a squabble regarding his inheritance. Now this may seem odd to us, but in the ancient world it was common for rabbis like Jesus to serve as mediators in disputes. Therefore, it wasn't unusual for Jesus as a leader in the Jewish community to be approached in this manner (Luke 12:13-14).

The brother who approached Jesus wasn't looking for a mediator or an arbitrator as much as he was looking for an advocate. He didn't want someone to help him *determine* what was fair as much as he wanted someone to tell him what he *already thought* was fair (Luke 12:13). The wording of the man's petition to Jesus implies that the split between him and his brothers had already taken place, and most likely the man was making a last ditch effort to get what he felt should be his. Rather than answer the man's concern, Jesus decided to tell a parable—a story to illustrate the principle He wanted to teach.

> **Read Luke 12:16-21 *aloud*. How many times did the rich man use the words "I," "my," or "me"? What conclusions can you draw about his attitude and intent based on that usage?**

> **Do you think the rich man was self-consumed before his banner farming year? Or do you think he became self-consumed afterward? What difference does it make?**

Encouraging His followers to be on their guard against all forms of greed, Jesus described a rich farmer whose crop was so abundant that he didn't have any place to store it. Rather than give away or sell the excess, he decided to tear down his barns and build larger ones where he could store all his grain and goods. His reasoning was simple: With all of his savings he could live a posh life of eating, drinking, and celebrating. But his life was about to end. God called the rich farmer a fool, one unable to determine what's truly important in life. That very night would be his last, and all his abundance would go to someone else.

The parable is a colorful portrait of the outcome of a selfish life and a reminder that our possessions are never meant to possess us. With

Jesus refused to judge on behalf of either brother in the conflict (Luke 12:13-21). Instead, Jesus focused His attention on the core issue of the matter —greed.

Watch the teaching segment "Recognizing That Everything Has Its Season" from the *Scouting the Divine* DVD to see Margaret discuss how to recognize and embrace the different stages of life. You can watch the video during your *Scouting the Divine* study group or download it for yourself at *margaretfeinberg.com*.

"Do not store up for yourselves treasures on earth, where moth and rust destroy, and where thieves break in and steal. But store up for yourselves treasures in heaven, where neither moth nor rust destroys, and where thieves do not break in or steal; for where your treasure is, there your heart will be also" (Matthew 6:19-21).

everything God gives, we have a responsibility to use what we've been entrusted with as good stewards. Ultimately, we are accountable to God for what we own—and that's a good thing.

When we choose to use what we've been given wisely, greed dissipates. The wisdom of God will always challenge us to place everything before Him and use what we've been given in a way He desires, which at times will mean emptying our silos for others.

What do the silos look like in your life?

Have you ever had a time in life when you emptied a portion of your silo for someone else? What was the result?

How are you changed in the process of giving? Do you find that giving reduces the number of "I," "my," and "me" in your life? Why or why not?

SOWING SEEDS

As we walked around the farm, I felt my stomach grumbling. I looked at the acres and acres of corn and asked Joe if I could grab a quick snack. He smiled. "You don't want that corn because it's feed corn for animals," he advised.

Despite Joe's warning, I picked some of the feed corn, shucked the green outer husk, and took a big bite. Though the corn looked similar to something I would purchase at the grocery store, it tasted starchy rather than sweet. As I spit it out, Joe gloated, "Told you!"

While still picking remnants of feed corn from my teeth, Joe invited me to ride the tractor. We rounded the corner of the barn and there sat Big John in all of its green glory. This was no ordinary tractor. This was a John Deere 8430. In the farming community, those numbers meant it had racing stripes. Since its tires were as tall as me, I was grateful for the

---

"Possessions are bonded to a deep, often irrational fear—the fear of one day not having enough. Regardless of how much wealth is squirreled away, this gnawing fear presses frail humans to acquire more. There is never quite enough because the insecurity within never dies."[9]
—Kenneth Bailey,
author and lecturer

On a farm, it's easy to see the diligence and hard work of a farmer. To discover some spiritual insights about this principle, read section 2.5, "It All Comes Out in the Field," in the *Scouting the Divine* book.

According to Hickory Hill Farms, LLC *(hickoryhillfarmsllc.com)*, one bushel of corn can sweeten more than 400 cans of Coca-Cola.

steps as I scrambled inside. Joe and I scrunched together on the seat as he carefully explained all the gears.

My legs were too short to reach the pedals, so Joe and I shared a seat and began making laps around the farm. As he drove, we talked about life, faith, and even the Bible.

One of the devices on the dashboard caught my attention. Joe explained that the machine helped his uncle control the seed population during the planting season. Based on the type of soil, his uncle adjusted the amount of seed distributed.

"Aaron knows his field so well that he knows exactly where to bump up the seed dial on the most fertile land," Joe said. "He knows if he spends a few extra dollars on seed in the right areas, the crop will be even larger."

"Sounds like the parable of the sower," I said.

"I think about that a lot," Joe said. "If Uncle Aaron knows his land so well that he knows just the right amount of seeds to release at just the right time of year to bring a fruitful harvest, how much more does God know you and me?"

Right on, Joe. In Jesus' story, a farmer planted seeds. As he planted, some of the seeds toppled out of the bag and the birds ate them. Others poured out on rocky terrain, and the seeds sprouted, but because the soil lacked depth, the tender plants died in the heat of the day. Other seeds fell among thorns that robbed them of the nutrients they needed to survive. Those plants survived but failed to yield any fruit. Still others were sprinkled on good ground. Not only did these healthy plants sprout and survive, but they also thrived, producing an exponentially fruitful crop.

> **Read Mark 4:1-20. How would you describe a heart that is like rocky soil? Thorny soil? Shallow soil?**

> **Think about good soil. What are the characteristics of a heart in which God's Word can survive and thrive?**

Even if you don't have a farm, you can still enjoy the fun of harvest. Some farms allow you to pick your own fruits, nuts, and berries when they're ripe. Take a look at *pickyourown. org* to find one near you.

The Bible contains nearly three dozen references to plowing and more than 300 to fields.

The parable of the sower appears in Matthew and Luke, as well as Mark. In all three Gospels, it is the beginning parable in a series of parables and is also the key to understanding the parables coming behind it since it deals primarily with how individuals receive the call of Christ.

Listen to the audio segment called "Meet Joe the Farmer" this week. Your group leader will send it to you via e-mail, or you can download it at *margaretfeinberg.com*. These audio recordings are designed to help you connect more deeply with the Good Shepherd as you spend time Scouting the Divine.

The narrative of the Bible takes place in an agrarian dominated context from Genesis through the Gospels. It isn't until the adventures of Paul and the early church that we find the Scripture consistently speaking into and out of a more urban context.

Consider each of the following areas of spiritual living listed below. When it comes to your receptivity of these particular areas, would you consider the soil of your heart fruitful, rocky, thorny, or shallow?

• Bible study _____

• Prayer _____

• Church _____

• Personal holiness _____

• Service _____

• Discipling others _____

Which spiritual discipline or practice is most fruitful in your life? Which do you tend to struggle with more?

What steps can you take to prepare the soil of your heart for growth in these areas?

FARMING AND THE BIBLE

We spent the rest of the afternoon hanging out on the farm. After a dinner of greasy burgers and the biggest plates of French fries I've ever seen at a local diner named "Bob's," we set out to meet the famous Uncle Aaron I'd been hearing so much about.

After a warm greeting, we all sat around the kitchen table and talked about life, farming, and the Bible. In preparing for my visit with Joe and Aaron, I discovered more than a hundred Scripture passages that described the process of reaping and harvesting, but those only scratched the surface of what the Bible has to say about farming.

In the genesis of creation, God created the heavens and the earth. In the mystery of our planet's conception, light separated from darkness, and sky separated from water. On the third unforgettable day, land and sea detached. The first dry ground appeared and promptly produced vegetation. In what's described as a single day, God created soil, water sources, and reproductive plant life.

The following day brought order and time through the creation of the sun, moon, and corresponding seasons. The fifth day filled the ocean with living creatures beyond imagination. On the sixth day God filled the earth with animals and, finally, created Adam and Eve to rule over the earth and all its creatures. Then God rested.

Filled with literary beauty, the creation story circles themes of time, weather, and agriculture. In Genesis 2, we learn that God formed human life "of dust from the ground," demonstrating the deep connection between the earth and humanity. Adam and Eve's initial assignment from God was to care for that which springs out of the ground—the garden.

After a tragic moment of willful disobedience, the assignment became exponentially more difficult. Cultivating the land now required sweat, pain, and hard work. Thorns, weeds, pestilence, disease, and drought—all foreign concepts before sin entered the picture—became everyday struggles in the fields. Eden, the paradise we've been longing for ever since, was gone.

Yet God continued (and continues) to call His children to care for and be connected to the earth. Scripture is deeply rooted in agricultural themes. Throughout the Old Testament, harvest represents abundance, the reward for labor, and a testimony of God's goodness and blessing. When Isaac sowed seed in his land, he reaped a hundredfold in his harvest. Scripture is quick to note that the Lord blessed him (Genesis 26:12). Even the shepherd king, David, called on God for abundance and blessing in the harvest. He petitioned God that the barns would be full with every type of produce (Psalm 144:13).

Meanwhile, images of failed harvests were used by many of the prophets to symbolically represent God's judgment or the people's unwillingness to follow God's law (Isaiah 17:11; Jeremiah 8:20). Ancient societies were particularly attuned to the harvest because its fruitfulness was often a matter of life and death. Rain, drought, fire, and enemies didn't just threaten a crop but the people's survival, making the topic of harvest fertile ground for teaching and instruction (1 Samuel 12:17; Judges 6:4-5; Job 31:12; Amos 4:7). God used three years of famine to get David's attention so that he sought the face of the Lord once again (2 Samuel 21:1), and Job's testing included severe harvest losses (Job 1).

Three particularly significant festivals were based on the agrarian calendar. Passover coincided with the barley harvest (Leviticus 23), the Feast of Pentecost (also known as the Feast of Weeks) celebrated the

The life and celebrations of the Jewish people often centered around harvests. Throughout the Bible, time is identified by a particular harvest. For example, Ruth and Naomi arrived in Bethlehem "at the beginning of barley harvest" (Ruth 1:22). While these mentions of time-keeping are easy to miss, they point to the life of a people embedded in an agrarian culture.

Harvest points to the natural rhythm of our world. After the flood, God promised that as long as the earth remains, humanity will experience "seedtime and harvest, and cold and heat, and summer and winter, and day and night" (Genesis 8:22). In the Book of Ecclesiastes, one of the darker philosophers of the Bible, Solomon, reminisced on such patterns and the promise that for everything there is a season.

Pentecost has many names in the Bible including the Feast of Weeks, the Feast of Harvest, and the Latter Firstfruits. In Hebrew, it's known as Shavuot and celebrated on the 50th day after Passover. To learn more about the Feast of Pentecost, read Leviticus 23:1-16.

Land is frequently associated with the blessings and promises of God. Consider the covenant God made with Abraham in Genesis 12. Not only did God promise Abraham too many descendants to count, but He also promised a land in which those descendants could live.

Scripture reminds us that what we sow, we will reap—a principle taught in Job, one of the oldest books of the Bible: "Those who plow iniquity and those who sow trouble harvest it" (Job 4:8). That which we plant will come to fruition. If we plant good seed, then we will harvest a good crop, but planting bad seed will yield a bad crop.

wheat harvest (Exodus 34:22), and the Feast of Booths (Exodus 23:16) lined up with the fruit harvest. In addition, the Feast of First Fruits was based on an agricultural practice of farmers bringing a portion of their first produce to the priests (Leviticus 23:9-14). Even to this day, the Book of Ruth—a story about redemption as well as seasons and harvest—is often read during the Feast of Pentecost.

Walking through fields with His disciples, the master storyteller Jesus used metaphors and images of planting and harvesting—themes those living in an agrarian society immediately grasped—to teach spiritual lessons.

What has been your experience with farming? Growing your own produce? What do you enjoy about the process?

Have you ever learned a spiritual lesson or seen one reflected through your farming or gardening experience? If so, describe.

Why do you think God relates so closely to the land and farming?

Does God's concern for the land tell you anything about His character? If so, what?

WHEAT AND TARES

I was curious about Aaron's roots. He shared the story of how he grew up on a small farm and a few years after high school began leasing his own acreage. Aaron focused on growing beans, corn, alfalfa, and wheat. "It gets in your blood," Aaron said with a rugged confidence. "What's sad is that even though my family was farm-oriented, I'm the only one left farming full-time. It's a sign that farming has gotten so tough—especially with the cost of land."

Yet Aaron loved farming and continued doing it despite the lean years and hardship. As we talked, I recognized that Aaron easily—almost naturally—connected with the harvest metaphors of Jesus. I took him to the story of the tares that were planted in a wheat field by an enemy (Matthew 13:24-30,36-43). The parable is one of the few that Jesus explained in detail to His followers. He defined the one who sows the good seed as the Son of Man, the field as the world, the good seeds as those of the kingdom, and the tares as those of the evil one. At the end of the age, the Son of Man will send forth His angels to gather the tares and throw them into the fire, but the good seed—the righteous—will live vibrantly forever.

"As a farmer, what does this mean to you?" I asked.

"I interpret the tares as plants with no seed in them," Aaron said. "If you're just walking through a field and looking at them, then you can take for granted that it's good seed. But if you take them and roll them in your fingers, you'll find that some do have good seed. Others have nothing at all. They're empty husks. You won't see it in fields, but it always shows up in the grain tank. The chaff comes off and with a light wind, everything disappears that isn't the good seed."

Things started clicking into place. Didn't John the Baptist talk about how the Promised One would gather up the wheat into the barn but burn up the chaff (Matthew 3:12)?

"Like Aaron said," Joe piped in. "You can't tell wheat from chaff just by looking at it. You have to grab, squeeze, and crush it to find out whether it's real or not. I think that's true of the spiritual life. Some people can look really good on the outside—they can seem more mature or look like they really know their Bible—but when it comes to the pressure of life and getting crushed, that's when the fruit really shows."

My mind flashed to moments when I'd seen this principle play out in people's lives, and I felt the pang of those memories. I've known people who, because of the temptations or pressures of life, bailed on their faith completely. I've also seen those who, despite Job-like trials and temptations, held onto God, goodness, and faith.

The parable of the wheat and tares is found in Matthew 13:24-30. A "tare" is a type of weed that looks like wheat when it's growing but is poisonous if eaten.

"Even if I knew that tomorrow the world would go to pieces, I would still plant my apple tree."[10]
—Martin Luther

Read Job 1:13–2:13. In the space below, make a list of all the things Job lost. How did he respond?

When was the last time you watched someone's true character and faith shine in times of difficulty and hardship?

Why do you think people's true selves are revealed during adversity?

Sometimes we plant something that doesn't reap an immediate harvest. One example is the planting of a tamarisk tree in Beersheba as described in Genesis 21. Abraham and Abimelech had a bumpy relationship until they decided to make a covenant to deal honestly and with kindness toward each other. After they made the commitment, Abraham planted a tamarisk tree, renowned for its cool shade in the desert.

The planting is a portrait of faith and trust, a deliberate choice to invest in something that won't yield an immediate return but will be enjoyed by generations to come. Even to this day, tamarisk trees are found in the vicinity of Beersheba, a reminder that what we plant may take on a life longer and greater than we imagined.

SEASONS

One of the passages that caught my attention was Genesis 8:21-22. After Adam and Eve's disobedience in the garden, God cursed the ground (Genesis 3:17-19) and promised that only through painful toil would Adam and his descendents enjoy the food of the land. Yet after Noah's faithful act of obedience, God promised to never again curse the ground on account of man or destroy every living thing:

"The LORD smelled the soothing aroma; and the LORD said to Himself, 'I will never again curse the ground on account of man, for the intent of man's heart is evil from his youth; and I will never again destroy every living thing, as I have done. While the earth remains, seedtime and harvest, and cold and heat, and summer and winter, and day and night shall not cease'" (Genesis 8:21-22).

"One of God's promises is seedtime and harvest, cold and heat, and summer and winter," I said. "You experience that day in and day out."

"We sure do," Aaron said. "And even though the seasons and days have a pattern, you don't often know what is going to happen next. When I read that passage I can't help but think of God's mercy."

"How so?" I asked.

"Well, even for the farmer who doesn't take good care of his fields, God still provides sunlight and rain. Even if the farmer doesn't believe in God, He still shows His grace. And if you have a bad year and your crop goes terrible, every spring is a new chance—you can try again."

I'd never seen the passage from Genesis from that perspective. I couldn't help but think about my life and the many times I grow frustrated with the season I'm in—not recognizing that it's just a season. This, too, will pass.

I'll be in the middle of a winter season and wonder why I'm not budding with new life. Or in the middle of fall harvest and wonder why I'm not getting enough rest. Or in the middle of spring and wonder why there's so much change. Or in the middle of summer and wonder why everything feels so dry.

> **Read Ecclesiastes 3:1-8. Reflecting on your life, what season do you think you're in right now: spring, summer, fall, or winter? Why?**

Not every year is a banner year for the farm. To read more about how Aaron handles tough times, check out section 2.10, "Low Yields," in the *Scouting the Divine* book.

> **Are you content with the season you're in? Why or why not? What contributes to any sense of discontentment you may feel?**

GLEANING

One of the laws from the Levitical code I've always found fascinating forbade farmers from harvesting the edges of the field. The prohibition ensured the poor and those in need could glean enough to live.

I read aloud the instructions in Leviticus:

"I do not at all understand the mystery of grace—only that it meets us where we are but does not leave us where it found us."[11]
—Anne Lamott

"Now when you reap the harvest of your land, you shall not reap to the very corners of your field, nor shall you gather the gleanings of your harvest" (Leviticus 19:9).

"When you reap the harvest of your land, moreover, you shall not reap to the very corners of your field nor gather the gleaning of your harvest; you are to leave them for the needy and the alien. I am the LORD your God" (Leviticus 23:22).

What differences do you see between these two passages? Do those differences mean anything to you?

Gleaning is not just an ancient practice. Organizations across the world support the hungry through gleaning. Volunteers head out to a farmer's field and pick the leftover produce. Then, the food is delivered to the needy. Check out *endhunger.org* to see if there is a collection going on in your area.

I was always intrigued by the closing of the command in the second Leviticus verse, "I am the LORD your God."

"What does this passage say about God? And us?" I asked.

Joe explained that while in our society there aren't official gleaners—those who survive on the leftovers of a field—like there were in ancient times or like there are today in other areas of the world, the same principle still applies. Once Aaron noticed some guys walking his fields after the harvest, picking up leftover ears of corn and tucking them into their oversized pockets.

"Aaron just let them have it," Joe said. "He figured they needed it to feed their chickens."

Joe pointed out that what those guys were doing was still work. In tending the field, it's not just the farmer who had to work hard, but the gleaners, too, as they gathered the leftovers. "What that says about God is that He has blessed us with so much," Joe said. "And we need to leave some for those who aren't as fortunate so they can receive a blessing from God, too. But the deeper issue here is a heart one."

"What do you mean?" I asked.

"I think God wants us to understand that we don't need all that we think we do," Joe said. "There are years we'll set a goal for so many bushels but end up short after harvesting. Sometimes if we were to go glean and clean up the corners and scraps on every field, then we'd make up the difference. The principle of gleaning reminds us that even if we didn't hit our goals, we'll still survive. Gleaning teaches us that it's not about having more, it's about having enough."

What are some modern equivalents of gleaning? Have you ever participated in any of these activities? Describe your experience.

Think about all the elements of your life—relationships, entertainment, work, and others. Assuming these areas of life are fields, what does it mean for you to plow them to the edges? How would your life look different if you left the edges unplowed?

In what ways does gleaning make you more dependent on God—both as the person who leaves the extra in the field and the one who gathers it? In what ways is gleaning an expression of the character of God?

LEARNING TO WAIT ON GOD

By the time I left Aaron and Joe, I was grateful we made the trip and for the spiritual insights I garnered along the way. Through my time on the farm, I was reminded that everything in life has its season. Though I may be tempted to wish I were living in another season of life, the best possible life begins with contentment and a recognition that God has me at the right place at the right time. Our discussion of gleaning reminded me that in a culture that lends itself to efficiency and productivity, God calls us to be intentional about generosity, always increasing our dependence on Him.

Go online and share something you learned from this session using #scoutingthedivine.

Lord, I am thankful that You are the Alpha and the Omega—the beginning and the end. I am grateful that You organize my days and my years in such a way that You'll be most glorified. Father, help me to embrace contentment in every area of my life. Help me to celebrate where You've placed me today and to walk in the hope and confidence that the good work You've begun will come to full fruition. Father, help me to walk in the humility necessary to glean when I'm in need and in generosity when I have the opportunity to provide for others who are in need. Let me be a vessel of Your love. In Jesus' name, amen.

ACTIVITY

Plant something new. Visit your local greenhouse or hardware store, and purchase some seeds, soil, and a small container. Talk to an employee about what might grow best in your area. Consider planting fresh spices, flowers, vegetables, or even a fruit tree. Take time to water and nurture your plant's growth. As you do, reflect on the deeper work God wants to do in your life as you grow in the fullness of all He has called and created you to be.

SCRIPTURE MEMORY

"For I am confident of this very thing, that He who began a good work in you will perfect it until the day of Christ Jesus" (Philippians 1:6).

SCOUTING THE DIVINE

As you go through the upcoming week, pay attention to your calendar. Whether that's a traditional calendar, dayplanner, your iPhone calendar, or your Google calendar, look at the way you're spending your time. Are you in a spring, summer, fall, or winter season? Prayerfully consider what God is calling you to do in this season of your life. Spend some time reflecting on the last season you were in as well as the next season that God may have for you.

NOTES

SESSION
4

IN THE HIVE

Discovering a Land Overflowing with Honey

Friendship is one of the sweetest things in life. Not only do relationships compel you to try new things and expose you to fresh ideas, but they reveal things about God and yourself that you may not discover any other way.

My best friend, Leif, introduced me to Cross Bar X in Durango, Colorado, a few years ago, and to this day I remain grateful. While we were dating, Leif kept telling me about this special place where he served as a counselor for three summers. For him, the camp was a place of restoration and healing.

While we were living in Alaska, Leif heard the camp needed a caretaker for a weekend so the staff could take a brief mid-summer retreat. He jumped at the chance to return, and I went with him.

The emerald grass that once covered the surrounding valley had turned amber under hot arid days. As we rounded the gravel driveway into the camp, I was struck by the visible difference between the camp property and the rest of the land. Lush grass—and the life it symbolized—carpeted the fields. A handful of cabins lined the left side of a large green field. Larger log lodges were on the right. Horses stood at attention in their corral. Goats and sheep poked their noses through the wire mesh gate. Against the background of the valley, Cross Bar X represented a place of hope.

))) To learn more about the vision and ministry at Cross Bar X, visit *crossbarxcamp.org*.

"Pure and undefiled religion in the sight of our God and Father is this: to visit orphans and widows in their distress, and to keep oneself unstained by the world" (James 1:27).

))) Map out some one-of-a-kind stops for your next road trip with the help of *roadsideamerica.com*.

Sporting a deep tan and bright smile, Nick welcomed us into his home and introduced me to his wife, Tracy, and their four daughters. Over the course of the evening, I learned more about the camp, but what I found most intriguing was Nick's approach to ministry. Not only did he set out with a vision to reach low-income youth three decades ago, but he stayed true to that vision. He committed his life, his family, his everything to fulfill that purpose. Listening to Nick and Tracy exchange stories with us, I knew that for many kids, Cross Bar X is truly the highlight of their year—a place they come to have fun, try new things, and enjoy the love and care of counselors, while also being introduced to Jesus.

By the time we left, I knew we'd be back. Since that first trip, Leif and I have returned to the camp many times. One evening while spending time with Nick and his family, the conversation circled around to our recent trip to visit Lynne in Oregon.

"Besides the shepherdess, who do you want to interview?" Nick asked.

"I'm still trying to narrow the list down," I said. "But I've already started researching for my next one—a beekeeper."

"Durango happens to be the home of Honeyville," Nick said. "One of the suppliers is a friend of the camp."

I instantly recognized the name, Honeyville, as a place we had stopped on an earlier trip to Durango. I love all things Americana and can't resist pulling off the highway to explore touristy sites with odd claims like "The world's largest round barn," "Home of the two-headed calf," or "See 'The Lord's Prayer' written on a grain of rice." These curiosity stops make road trips unforgettable. My favorite pit stops involve food, which is why we couldn't resist Honeyville. The factory store featured specialty honeys, jams, jellies, and sauces—all with free samples.

"Gary said he'd be glad to see you, so just give him a call," Nick instructed.

After a brief introduction, Gary graciously invited me to visit. We set up a time the following day. The hour-long drive to Lewis, Colorado, was nothing short of spectacular. Nestled in the San Juan mountains, the land was a slow-brewed blend of rolling hills, rugged peaks, and rocky crests. After a left-hand turn onto a gravel road, I knew I was nearing the driveway to Gary's home.

The address Gary had given me over the phone matched the metal numbers hanging on a slanted post. I looked across the field and noticed a wide barn standing nearly a quarter of a mile from the road. As I turned into the driveway, potholes jarred the car reminding me to drive slower. Each side of the narrow road boasted sage-colored fields with hay bales spaciously strewn throughout. Against a bluebird sky, the serene scene made me long for simpler days and a slower pace.

As I neared the white barn, a man wearing a long-sleeved blue shirt, khaki pants, and well-worn leather boots greeted me on a four-wheeler.

"You Margaret?"

I nodded.

"I'm Gary," he said. "Ma'am, follow me this way."

Something about the "ma'am" caught me off guard—especially since Gary was decades older than me. Yet over the course of the afternoon, I found the phrase endearing—a welcome reminder of the respect all too often lost between generations.

Parking his four-wheeler near the entrance to the warehouse, I followed him into the large building. My nostrils flared at the sickly sweet smell of honey. Bees darted through the air, landing to feast on any sugary residue they could find.

As I looked around the warehouse, I noticed green and white wooden boxes stacked from floor to ceiling. Though a few rogue bees buzzed around, I was confident they were mostly empty.

"Nick tells me you've been doing this for awhile," I said.

Without realizing it, I had just tapped into this man's greatest passion: beekeeping. Gary explained how he grew up in Durango and married his high school sweetheart. Flat broke, they decided to move to California for a job. Gary's in-laws followed. One night at dinner Gary's father-in-law announced, "I met the most fascinating man today. He's a beekeeper, and I watched him extract honey."

Gary wanted to go see for himself. After work the next day, he went over to the beekeeper's and knocked on the door. When no one answered, Gary cracked the door only to discover a room full of bees.

According to the American Beekeeping Federation (*abfnet. org*), the number of keepers who produce more than 6,000 pounds of honey annually has declined from 2,054 in 2005 to about 1,100 in 2008.

Over the centuries, selective breeding by beekeepers has created honeybees that produce far more honey than the colony of bees actually needs. The keepers harvest the extra honey for sale.

In 2006, the term "colony collapse disorder" became widely known. It describes the sudden rise of bee deaths and hive collapses in the United States and Europe. In a single winter, Gary lost nearly 1,000 hives. Scientists are still trying to fully understand the sudden death of the bees.

"Come on in," a friendly voice invited.

"I was so fascinated by what this man was doing that I followed him around for the next two and a half years. I'd help him make equipment like these panels, put in the queens, and start new hives. Anything I learned about beekeeping I learned from him."

In 1969, Gary bought 53 hives and eventually built them up to 300. "I was still working my milkman route and caring for the bees. My wife forced me to make a decision: go into beekeeping full-time or work as a milkman. The decision was tough—especially since the milk route was a union job and provided medical, dental, and vision coverage. I knew what I had to do."

Gary sold the 300 hives to his best friend and worked full-time as a milkman.

"I was the most miserable person," Gary recalled.

Ten months later Gary's wife concluded the new scenario wasn't working. Gary purchased 200 hives and launched out on his own as a full-time beekeeper. His first hives were full of disease. Most of them died the first winter, but Gary managed to hold onto the business. He eventually built up to 3,200 hives with 75,000 bees in each hive at his peak. Eventually, Gary and his family moved back to Colorado. Today, Gary and his son work to maintain their 2,000 hives.

As Gary spoke, I could see how the years in business as a beekeeper had taken a toll on his body, but not his spirit. Spending time with someone who is passionate about their work is infectious, and though some of the details he shared about the hives seemed superfluous, the enthusiasm with which he shared them kept me intrigued.

Like Gary, everyone has a story. Why is it important to listen to other people's stories? What do you gain from learning and listening to others about their personal and professional journeys?

What are the advantages to being passionate about what you do? What are the disadvantages?

Do you think being passionate about something is contagious? Why or why not? What are you most passionate about?

"Are these the hives?" I asked, pointing to the stacks of boxes.

"They're hives, but they're not active," Gary explained.

Gary reached into one of the wooden boxes stacked with inch-wide brown panels. The panel he extracted was lined with a dark honeycomb. Only a few of the six-cylinder combs on the panel had lids; the others remained empty. Though Gary claimed the hives were inactive, bees still lined the frames consuming both the wax and honey. Gary pointed to a single hole on the side of the boxes and explained that if the hive was alive, the only dangerous place to be would be in front of that single entrance and exit to the hive.

He explained how the bees are wired to return to the exact same place where their hive is located. If Gary takes one of his boxed hives and simply rotates the box 90 degrees, the bees gathering the pollen and water may take anywhere from an afternoon to a few days to find the entrance to the hive. If Gary moved the hive more than one-half mile from its location, the bees would probably never find their hive again. That's why when he moves a hive he usually does it at night—when the bees are most likely to be inside.

What biblical allusions to bees or honey can you think of? What are your general thoughts surrounding those images?

Did you know you can replace up to half of the sugar called for in a recipe with honey? If you're baking, *ThomasHoney.com* advises that for each cup of honey used, reduce the liquid called for in the recipe by ¼ cup and add ¼ to ¾ teaspoons of baking soda. In addition, lower the oven temperature by 25 degrees to reduce the chance of burning or over-browning whenever using honey.

According to The National Honey Board *(honey.com)*, modern beehives usually consist of a series of square or rectangular wooden boxes without tops or bottoms placed one on top of another. Inside the boxes, frames are hung in parallel, in which bees build up the wax honeycomb where they both raise their young and store honey.

What spiritual lessons do you think you could learn from looking at a hive?

The largest bee in a colony is the queen bee. She is fed royal jelly—a secretion from the glands of young workers that allows her to become sexually mature. Rather than having a horizontal cell like many of the bees in the hive, her cell is specially constructed as vertical and larger than the normal brood comb.[13]

THE WONDER OF THE HIVE

Gary described the three different types of bees in a hive.

Queen bee: Her role is to go on a flight at the beginning of her career in which she is impregnated by the drones. On average, she will lay 1,000 to 2,000 eggs per day.

Drones: The life mission of these male bees is to accompany the queen bee on her maiden flight and impregnate her. Afterward, they will be booted from the hive and die.

Worker bees: It's estimated that 98 percent of the bees in a given hive are worker bees. The worker bees perform a variety of tasks including:

The drones, or male bees of the hive, have eyes twice the size of the other bees. Because they're designed to mate with the queen bee in flight, they use their better vision to locate the queen. Also, drones don't have stingers.

- *Attendant bees* care for the queen, ensuring she is well fed and her needs are met.
- *Cleaning bees* clean the cells for the arrival of larvae.
- *Nurse bees* care for the young larvae.
- *Pollen gathering bees* collect pollen in the basket-like holsters on their back legs and deliver it to the hive, where it's used to develop the brood.
- *Sealing bees* seal the honeycomb containing the honey.
- *Drone feeding bees* provide food for the drones.
- *Honeycomb bees* build the waxy structure that stores the honey and that bees call home.
- *Mortuary bees* remove the dead bees from the hive so disease doesn't spread.
- *Fanning bees* flap their wings so that the hive can maintain a consistent temperature.
- *Water carrying bees* deliver water to the hive to maintain the bees' survival.
- *Guard bees* ensure that the hive is safe from predators— including bees from other hives—who may want to steal the valuable honey.

On the back of their hind legs, bees collect pollen that they in turn use as a protein for help in raising their young.

The hive is literally abuzz with activity. It's estimated that during the summer, the worker bees travel more than 55,000 miles just to gather enough nectar to produce a single pound of honey. Over the course of their lifetime, worker bees will only produce about $\frac{1}{12}$ of a teaspoon of honey and $\frac{1}{80}$ of a teaspoon of wax.

"I had no idea all that went on inside a hive," I said.

"These are some of the most incredible creatures you'll ever encounter," Gary said.

How does knowing some of these intricacies affect the wonder or awe you feel for God?

What kinds of things naturally leave you in wonder or awe of God?

As Gary described all of the inner workings of the hive, I was given a glimpse of how within a bee community everything comes together for the good of the hive. The parallels between the hive and the body of Christ surfaced.

When every person fulfills their role with due diligence, something wonderful happens that can't be manufactured any other way. A hive is a community of tens of thousands of bees working together for one common purpose. Is the church much different?

If a community of bees accomplishes so much with so little, how much more can you and I accomplish together? Bees face countless challenges with variances in weather, wind, and vegetation, yet through diligence produce something that can't be manufactured any other way. Real honey has no substitutes, and neither does the body of Christ.

Beeswax was used as plastic during ancient times. It has been found in Egyptian tombs and was used in ancient Roman paper, Egyptian shipbuilding, and Greek metal casting.

"If I could take time with any atheist or unbeliever, put on the whole beekeeper protective clothes, sit down with them in front of a hive, and pull out the frames and explain how it all works together, I don't think that person would leave without being convinced that God was behind it all. So many things have to come into play before those bees make one drop of honey."
—Gary, the beekeeper

Read 1 Corinthians 12:1-26 *aloud*. What parallels can be drawn between a hive and this passage?

What parallels can be drawn between your own Christian community and this passage?

Reflect on the different roles of the bees within the hive. Which one best describes the gifts you feel like you bring to a community?

Do you tend to view your contribution to the body of Christ as less important, essential, or extremely important? Why?

What is the most amazing thing you've seen a group of followers of Jesus accomplish when they work together for God's glory?

What holds you back from truly being yourself and using the gifts God has given you? Who loses when you hold back?

SWEET SCRIPTURES

Gary gave me a full tour of the facility. The large warehouse was stacked with a variety of supplies. In addition to the hives, I noted large containers used to store honey. Boxes of jars of honey lined the wall. In the back room, a large industrial machine was used to automate the process of extraction by separating the wax and producing pure honey. Each room was filled with an overpoweringly sweet smell that was both repulsive and enticing to the nose all at the same time.

We walked into a small room reserved for making bees wax candles. The candles lined the shelves in all different shapes and forms. There were pinecones, corn, crosses, and even a Santa Clause figurine. I picked one up and felt the soft wax against my fingers.

We sat down next to the worktable. Prior to our trip, I researched honey and bees in Scripture. Honey is a rich, nutrient-filled food mentioned throughout the Bible. Nearly two-dozen references throughout the Old Testament describe the promised land as a place "flowing with milk and honey."

David and his people received honey (among other foods) while surviving in the wilderness and hiding from Saul (2 Samuel 17:26-29). Jeroboam's wife took cake, loaves, and a jar of honey on her travels (1 Kings 14:3). Honey was even part of the tithe.

> **Read 2 Chronicles 31:4-6. Why do you think honey was included as part of the offering?**

The Hebrew word used for honey appears more than 50 times in the Old Testament and has been translated as "bee's honey" or "syrup." In antiquity, natural sugars were produced by fruits like dates or apricots as well as in the honey produced by bees. The idea that bees were domesticated to some extent is conveyed in 2 Chronicles 31:5, regarding the first fruit offerings.

A recent excavation in northern Israel revealed a 3,000-year-old beekeeping operation dating back to the time of King David. Some scholars argue that the Israelites made honey exclusively from figs and dates, but such archaeological finds confirm that beekeeping is an ancient practice.[15]

Not only does Scripture describe the flavor of honey, but it also mentions the smell. The burnt offerings of ancient days were often described in terms of their pleasantness or sweetness. After Noah exited the ark, he built an altar and offered a series of burnt offerings described as a sweet or pleasing aroma, which some believe to be comparable to honey (Genesis 8:20-21). Despite the fragrance, God's real assessment of an offering always rested in the condition of the heart.

The judgments of the Lord are described as "sweeter also than honey and the drippings of the honeycomb" (Psalm 19:9-11). David, the shepherd king, described God's words as "sweeter than honey"

(Psalm 119:103). Solomon warned that an adulteress' lips drip honey that in the end turns bitter (Proverbs 5:3-4), but later on describes his own bride's lips as dripping with honey, too (Song of Solomon 4:10-12).

Honey was one of the foods that helped save the lives of 10 men as described in Jeremiah (Jeremiah 41:7-8). And one of John the Baptist's keynote characteristics was that his diet consisted of honey and locusts (Matthew 3:3-4).

> **"Honey" is used in both a positive and negative context in the above biblical passages. Why do you think it's appropriate in each of those situations?**

Google "The Beehives of Tel Rehov" to learn about an incredible archaeological find of ancient domesticated bees.

To learn more about bees and honey, visit the National Honey Board at *honey.com*.

THE KING WHO LOST HIS CROWN

I decided to ask Gary about another passage that bothered me. In 1 Samuel we read the story of Saul, who committed multiple blunders as a leader. He was selected as the first king of Israel after the people declared they wanted to have political leadership instead of the priestly leadership that set them apart from other nations. God gave the people exactly what they asked for in their first king, Saul, whose name can be translated "asked for."

Shortly after Saul became king of Israel, he took matters into his own hands. Rather than depending on God or obeying the prophet Samuel, he believed he could get things done better and more efficiently if he just did them on his own.

> **Read 1 Samuel 13:1-14. In this passage, how did Saul take matters into his own hands?**

> **How did Samuel respond? What did Saul lose as a result of his disobedience?**

While the Israelites engaged in a battle with the Philistines, Saul ordered his people not to eat under penalty of death until victory was declared. Saul's son, Jonathan, didn't hear the order before he entered the forest, where he discovered "honey on the ground" (1 Samuel 14:25). When the people saw the honey, no one tasted it except for Jonathan. He took his staff, dipped it into the honeycomb, and enjoyed the sweetness. Only then did a soldier inform Jonathan of his father's decree.

Though Jonathan openly admitted his error, Saul was merciless and the death penalty remained. But the people came to Jonathan's rescue—defending him to his own father—and saved his life.

Read 1 Samuel 14:24-52. Who do you think Saul lost respect from after he issued his decree not to eat?

"But the people said to Saul, 'Must Jonathan die, who has brought about this great deliverance in Israel? Far from it! As the LORD lives, not one hair of his head shall fall to the ground, for he has worked with God this day.' So the people rescued Jonathan and he did not die" (1 Samuel 14:45).

Who do you think Saul lost respect from after he issued the death of his own son?

Which of Saul's character traits are revealed in this story?

Saul ended up taking his own life during the Battle of Gilboa. He asked his armor-bearer to kill him, but the servant was too afraid, so Saul fell on his sword to kill himself. Read 1 Samuel 31 for the full story.

Saul's foolishness caused him to lose respect from everyone. The prophet Samuel lost respect for Saul as a leader when he tried to fulfill the priestly role by offering the sacrifice. The people lost respect for Saul when he issued a decree not to eat despite the fact they were at war. And Saul's own son, Jonathan, lost respect for his father when he would not offer grace, compassion, or reprieve after his innocent mistake. Folly marked Saul's days as king of Israel, and he faced conflict on every side.

Has honey in your pantry ever crystallized and transformed from a liquid to a solid before you could use it all? If so, simply place the container in warm water and it will transform back into a liquid.

If you haven't taken a photo of your group for Margaret's site, take one this week and send it to hello@margaretfeinberg.com!

Yet my question for Gary traced back to the description of the honey. "Would bees ever produce honey on the bare ground?" I asked, remembering what Scripture said Jonathan found in the forest.

Gary thought for a moment. "Heat could cause that," he finally said.

Gary explained that the design of the honeycomb is brilliant since a hexagon is one of the strongest shapes. Yet even with the six-sided construction, the honey inside is only supported by the wax, a naturally heat-sensitive substance. While water weighs 8 pounds per gallon, honey weighs 12 pounds per gallon. Though heat doesn't affect the weight of the honey, higher temperatures affect the strength of the wax.

A hive is designed so that it should never be above 96 degrees. In order to maintain a steady temperature, bees create their own air conditioning system by flapping their wings. On hot days, bees will go out and fill up one or both of their two stomachs with water. When they return to the hive, they'll regurgitate the water and then fan their wings to cool the hive. The problem arises when bees don't get enough water. Without the appropriate amount of water, they can't maintain the temperature of the hive.

"Since wax is the only thing supporting the heavy honey, it will naturally start to sag under the heat," Gary said. "Which could account for the honey running on the ground."

Reflecting on Gary's insight as a beekeeper, Saul's order seemed all the more foolish if not downright cruel. If what Gary described was true, then the armies were potentially fighting in extra hot weather with limited access to water. The insight was another reminder that Saul had let the crown go to his head and lost compassion for his people and those who defended him.

Based on these facts, how would you characterize Saul's leadership style?

What principles of leadership can you glean from this sort of explanation?

MILK AND HONEY

The first mention of the promised land as a place overflowing with milk and honey is in God's conversation with Moses near the burning bush. But in this account the "overflowing" of the honey isn't caused by heat but by an abundance of its treasured presence in the land promised to the Israelites.

> Read Exodus 3:1-9. Why do you think God described the promised land as a place overflowing with milk and honey? What was significant about this promise?

Canaan is the land between the Mediterranean Sea and the Jordan River—the promised land.

> The promised land could have been recognized for other details. Make a list of other characteristics of the promised land found in Deuteronomy 8:6-9 in the space below.

> Why do you think God chose to describe this land specifically as overflowing with milk and honey instead of another characteristic?

"The land which we passed through to spy out is an exceedingly good land. If the LORD is pleased with us, then He will bring us into this land and give it to us—a land which flows with milk and honey" (Numbers 14:7-8).

"As a beekeeper, what does it mean to you to say a land is overflowing with honey?" I asked.

"A land overflowing with honey is naturally bountiful," Gary explained. "It's a land that has everything you need and then some." He went on to say that for a land to be overflowing with honey means everything in that land works in its proper order. The winter snows don't melt too early or too late. The summer isn't too hot or too cold. Fall arrives at the right temperature and time. Why? Because if one of these elements is off—whether the temperature, timing of the seasons, precipitation, or weather—then the bees won't have the same window of opportunity to create and store their honey. Unless everything is working in its proper order, the land simply can't overflow with honey.

Gary's simple observation had profound meaning in my own life. God's promise to the Israelites was for a land where everything was in top working order. This was a place abounding in fruitful land and abundant vegetation. This was a land functioning in its proper rhythm as it was designed. How much I long for that in my own life! I want to live in the balance and blessing of everything working in its proper order—from my finances to my health to my relationships to my faith.

Do you feel like your own life is one marked by the promise of an overflow of milk and honey? Why or why not?

What words would you use as the defining characteristics of your life right now? What words do you wish you were using as the defining characteristics? What changes do you need to make to change your life?

What areas of your life are working in their proper order? What areas of your life are out of balance or out of control?

How would your life look different if everything was working in its proper order?

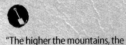

"The higher the mountains, the more understandable is the glory of Him who made them and who holds them in His hand."[16]
—Francis Schaeffer

"Hope is the only bee that makes honey without flowers."[17]
—Robert Green Ingersoll

Gary and I discussed many other passages that afternoon, and I still carry his words and wisdom with me. As I drove back toward the camp, I was grateful for my time with the beekeeper. Though the experience was far different from the weekend with the shepherdess, I found myself increasingly in awe of our God who pays attention to the minutest details.

OUR GOD IS INTRICATELY INVOLVED

All too often I read Scriptures like that of Jeremiah 29:11 which says that God knows His plans for us—to give us a future and a hope—with a kind of yeah-yeah attitude. Over the years, I've read, heard, and seen those types of passages so many times that their meaning has worn thin. Yet the wonders of the hive remind me that God really does pay attention to the tiniest of details. Indeed, God is more intricately involved than I ever imagined.

"'For I know the plans that I have for you,' declares the LORD, 'plans for welfare and not for calamity to give you a future and a hope'" (Jeremiah 29:11).

I also found a new sense of comfort in a verse I never fully understood before. Proverbs 27:7 says:

"A sated man loathes honey, but to a famished man any bitter thing is sweet."

Translating this into my modern world, I knew that someone who is truly full will always pass on dessert. Someone who is truly hungry will eat anything. The verse seemed practical and straightforward, like the one about a dog returning to its own vomit. But as I reflected on this verse, I thought of the other passages that compared God's Word to honey. And I was reminded of my prayer for spiritual hunger. Without hunger, we won't desire God or His Word. Yet when we sense that hunger, we must be wise in what we feast on. May the hunger to feast on God's Word become an eternal craving in your life.

Go online and share one lesson you've learned from this week's session using #scoutingthedivine.

Lord, Your ways are so far beyond and above our own. You pay attention to details our minds can't comprehend. The intricacies in something as simple as a beehive are amazing. If You care so much for the bees in the hive— how much more must You care for me? Father, awaken me to the reality of Your presence and tender care in my life. Help me slow down enough to see the ways You're working in and through me. And help me enter the land of blessing You've designed—one where things are in balance and working in their proper order as You intended. Help me glorify You with my life. In Jesus' name, amen.

ACTIVITY

Honey has many uses and can be fun to cook with. During the upcoming week, look for a recipe that includes honey. For some fresh ideas, google "honey" and "recipe." You'll find everything from breads to fruit dips. Commit to making one new recipe and sharing it with your community this week.

SCRIPTURE MEMORY

"For You formed my inward parts;
You wove me in my mother's womb.
I will give thanks to You, for I am fearfully and wonderfully made;
Wonderful are Your works,
And my soul knows it very well" (Psalm 139:13-14).

SCOUTING THE DIVINE

As you go through the upcoming week, consider the complexities of everyday items and activities. Beehives may seem simple from the outside, but the amount of work that goes into producing a single teaspoon of honey is amazing. So this week spend some time researching another aspect of the natural world and appreciate the wonders of God's handiwork. Consider selecting something native to your own area—such as a type of plant or flower—or go online to study the wonder of snow, rainbows, or even galaxies.

NOTES

AMONG THE VINEYARDS

Experiencing God's Tender Care

Where exactly does one find a winemaker? Maybe you know tons of vintners, but I didn't know any, and this perplexing question haunted me for six months.

I mentioned my desire to spend time with a winemaker to family, friends, and acquaintances I hoped wouldn't be bothered by the question. While many of them had visited vineyards (a few even offering to tag along as research assistants), none of them knew a vintner personally.

I wanted to find someone who had some sort of biblical framework in their background who could appreciate the wonder of Jesus' first miracle—turning water into wine—as well as Jesus' frequent use of a vineyard as the setting for His parables. I hoped to find someone who had taken Communion to comment on the beauty of the Son of God instructing His followers to drink the fruit of the vine in His remembrance.

After six months, I was still struggling to make any real connections with anyone—regardless of religious affiliation—in the wine industry. No one seemed able to help.

No one, except for Cathleen.

Are you on Facebook? You can find Margaret at *facebook.com/margaretfeinberg*. Become a fan of Threads while you're there.

Many believe the first cultivated grapes in California were grown by Spanish Franciscan friars who wanted to make a wine for the California Missions to use during Communion.

While catching up with my dear friend in a coffee shop in Chicago, I mentioned my need to her. "This shouldn't be that hard," I said, taken back by the exasperation in my own voice.

"My friend is a master vintner in Napa Valley," Cathleen said nonchalantly. Thanks to Facebook, by the end of the day I was electronically introduced to Kristof, and he graciously extended an invitation to visit Napa and learn more about his work. We scheduled a time in late February when the fields were dormant and he had a few afternoons to spare.

Leif and I touched down in Sacramento one late afternoon and enjoyed the hour-plus drive to the valley as the sun melted into the horizon. By the time we saw the signs for Napa, the silhouettes of the surrounding low-rise mountains were illuminated only by moonlight. Though beautiful by night, I longed for what daylight would bring.

Morning did not disappoint. Our 10 a.m. drive to meet Kristof was a breathtaking immersion into green beauty. We were surrounded by hills that boasted lush trees and bubbled up from the ground with ease, a sharp contrast to the pedicured vineyards below.

Leif followed the directions to one of the boutique Napa Valley vineyards where Kristof consults as a master vintner, ensuring their wines not only meet but exceed expectations. A thin sign marked the address of the private label vineyard and estate. We followed the narrow gravel road around a bend where we discovered a man I knew to be Kristof eating his lunch out of a plastic to-go container in the center of the circular driveway.

"What's for lunch?" I asked as a gentle greeting.

"Emergency Top Ramen," he said. "I always keep a few on hand."

I smiled. If Napa was known for its outstanding wines and gourmet food, then I was being given a backstage pass, ushered behind the scenes where the regular people live. Kristof's lack of presumption or airs was endearing; anyone who eats Top Ramen standing in the middle of the driveway is a friend of mine.

"I know a great place we could talk," Kristof offered. Leif and I followed him into a storage building lined with huge metal storage tanks and aging oak barrels. The rich smell of red wine filled my nostrils. We entered the main room and headed up a spiral staircase to a sitting room with built-in couches on every wall. Stickerless bottles were backlit on a shelf lining the ceiling, the soft orange hue transforming lowbrow glass containers into works of art.

"How did you end up here?" I asked, settling into one of the pillows on the couch.

Kristof explained that his grandparents had moved from Sweden to the United States and settled in California. He was raised with a European upbringing and developed an appreciation for fine food and wine early on. His appetite whetted, he decided to pursue a career as a chef, but at the last minute was persuaded by a family friend to pursue medicine and accepted a spot at a prestigious Christian college in Chicago.

During his sophomore year, he was challenged by an assignment to investigate a denomination outside of his Protestant background. He visited an Orthodox church and was taken by its deep appreciation for liturgy and history. Around the same time, he switched his major from pre-med to earn a double degree in business and art, and fell in love with a young woman named Jennifer, who, interestingly enough, shared his last name and the first name of his mother.

"So I went to Wheaton College to become a winemaker, embrace Eastern Orthodoxy, and meet my half-Swedish Californian wife with the same last name," Kristof said with a hearty laugh. "It's not your typical evangelical story."

"I love it!" I said, unable to hide a huge grin.

Like Kristof, we all have a story. What makes your story unique?

Why is it important to take time to listen to one another's stories? When was the last time you learned something about someone that really surprised you?

Watch the teaching segment "Experiencing God's Tender Care" from the *Scouting the Divine* DVD to see Margaret talk about experiencing the tender care of the Divine Vintner. You can watch the video during your *Scouting the Divine* study group or download it for yourself at *margaretfeinberg.com*.

Have you ever thought about the Bible as one story? If not, consider reading *A Million Miles in a Thousand Years* by Donald Miller to experience Scripture coming alive in new and fresh ways.

What biblical examples of the grapevine can you think of? How do you think meeting a vintner might change your perspective on those passages?

Listen to "New Way to Live" by Jason Gray from the *Scouting the Divine* playlist. Your group leader can e-mail you the whole playlist, or you can download it at *margaretfeinberg.com*.

TENDER CARE

Kristof explained that after graduation, he looked for employment. He contacted a family friend who had started a winery in Napa. "He didn't need anyone and neither did the next guy, but after following a laundry list of recommendations over the course of that week, I was eventually hired as a bottling supervisor," Kristof recalled.

"I didn't know the first thing about a winery, but since I had a college degree and was willing to work hard, the winemaker took notice, and I began working as a cellar rat," he recalled.

"Is that a promotion?" I asked.

"More of a lateral move," Kristof explained. "Cellar rats hook up hoses, clean things, and perform the hands-on manual labor that winemaking requires. In a kitchen it would be equivalent to a prep cook."

After his first harvest season, he became a "flying winemaker" and traveled to South Africa for their fall harvest season. He worked for a handful of wineries before landing a job in a premier wine lab where he studied enology—the science of wine. Eventually he moved up to be assistant to the head winemaker. In 2001, he created his first vintage. As a winemaker consultant, he now makes wine for four different labels.

Enology is the study of the aspects of wine and winemaking. Growing vines and harvesting grapes is considered viticulture—another science.

"Many of these small artisanal vineyards aren't large enough to hire full-time employees and instead choose to rely on highly experienced contract labor and professionals," Kristof explained.

"Like this winery?" I asked, pointing out the window to the vineyard below.

"Exactly," Kristof said. "And I love the smallness of it, because basically I'm a chef who grows his own ingredients. By being small I'm vertically integrated; in other words, nothing happens at any stage of the wine being made where I'm not involved in the decision."

"You look at every vine?" I asked.

"Not only that! I look at every cluster of grapes—at least once, but probably two, three, or even four times."

"That's a lot of tender care," I observed.

"Perhaps that's what it takes to be a good vintner."

Does anything surprise you about the care with which Kristof tends his vineyard? What are the first five words that come to mind when you think about his level of care?

Do you see any parallels between Kristof's care for the grapes and God's care for us? Explain.

Grapes grow in clusters of six to three hundred. The color of grapes ranges among crimson, black, dark blue, yellow, green, and pink.

WATER AND WINE

The image I had of the Napa Valley as a place of recreational gourmet play was a far cry from real life in the valley. I wondered what surprised people most about Napa.

"People are sometimes disappointed to discover that winemaking is nothing more than glorified farming," Kristof admitted. "I started before six o'clock this morning, and put in long hours throughout the year. If it weren't for the fact that we were fermenting grape juice into really great wine, no one would come to Napa. No one goes around visiting multi-million dollar chicken sheds or corn farmers to see how they farm.

Napa Valley features more than three hundred wineries and grows many different grape varieties. The area is visited by as many as five million people each year.

"Sometimes, in jest, when asked why I decided to become a winemaker, I reply, 'Since it was the first miracle in the Bible, it just seemed like a good idea!'"

That seemed like an open door to me, so I walked right through. I had read extensively about Jesus' miracle at Cana and learned that unlike most modern weddings in North America, weddings in ancient Israel were celebrated as feasts that lasted for up to a week. This required a significant commitment from the host family, who served large quantities of food and wine. In Hebrew culture, consumption of wine was part of a wedding celebration, though intoxication was unacceptable.

Read John 2:1-11. Several different people are involved in this parable. Make a list of each of the individuals in the space below. What role did each of them play?

Cana was a town in Galilee about four miles north of Nazareth. Today, a village called Kafr Kana claims to be the spot of Jesus' first miracle.

Who do you think was the most surprised by Jesus' miraculous display? Why?

What is significant about Jesus' ministry starting at a wedding?

Try a new recipe. Visit *cooks.com* and type in grape juice. Make a beverage, a salad, or a dessert you've never tried before.

From the description in John 2, Jesus' mother Mary was probably a friend or relative of the bride or bridegroom, and Jesus had been invited to the feast with the disciples. On the third day of the wedding—a note that hints at shadows of the third day of the resurrection and the banquet prophesied for the end of time—the servers noted that they were out of wine. This wasn't just a question of embarrassment; it was a crisis of honor, not to mention an enormous, unexpected financial expense.

At that moment, Mary turned to her son for help. Jesus' words, "Woman, what does that have to do with us? My hour has not yet come" (John 2:4), were prophetic because Jesus' time of suffering, death, and resurrection hadn't yet arrived. Unshaken by Jesus' inflexible response, Mary told the servants to blindly obey whatever Jesus commanded.

Jesus asked the servants to fill six stone ceremonial jars sitting nearby with water. The mention of the jars being made of "stone" signifies that they were for Jewish purification washings, since clay jars could be contaminated and therefore had to be destroyed according to rabbinic law.

Without any notable incident, trick, or display of power, Jesus told the servant to draw some water from the jars and take it to the headwaiter. Somewhere between the well and the palate something miraculous happened: Common water became choice wine.

The pronouncement by the headwaiter that this wine should have been served earlier is telling of the wine's quality. Interestingly, when Jesus performed His first miracle, He bypassed any restrictions of time. As Kristof later explained, wine takes years to make, beginning with prepping the soil, growing and pruning the vines, harvesting the grapes, collecting the juice, and then finally fermenting. When it comes to making great wine, time is your friend. Yet Jesus didn't need to wait.

Jesus' first miracle is about more than just fulfilling an immediate need or responding to His mom's insistence. John described the act as a "sign" (Greek *semeion*) rather than a "miracle" (Greek *dynamis*). The word choice conveys that the act disclosed something about God that had previously been hidden—namely, that Jesus was the Son of God who radiated the power and presence of His Father. The "miracle" at Cana was not so much a miracle as a revelation to His followers.

Why do you think Jesus' first miracle was turning water into wine?

Jesus' response might sound harsh to us, but "Woman, what does that have to do with us," was a common conversational phrase. The phrase was actually reassuring in the vernacular, a way of saying something like, "Don't worry. Leave it to me, and I'll take care of it in my own way."

The word used for the six jars Jesus ordered to be filled represents the Hebrew measure called the bath. A bath is equivalent to eight or nine gallons, so the jars were very large.

What was revealed about the character or mission of Jesus through this sign?

"What strikes you about the story of Jesus turning water into wine?" I asked Kristof.

"The idea of not bringing out the best wine until the end of an evening is still a phenomenon," he explained. "Some people assume this is an issue of sobriety, but it's also strange when you think about the tannins

Tannins are also found in tea, cranberries, pecans, and chocolate. To taste tannins, simply bite into an apple skin or a walnut. That dry bitterness you taste is typical of tannin. Or if you prefer, over steam a cup of hot tea. You'll recognize the tannins in the puckery taste.

Parallel accounts in Mark and Luke reveal that Jesus withdrew from the crowds across the lake only to find this huge crowd waiting for Him. Though the disciples were tired and wanted Him to send the people away, Jesus was moved with compassion and fed them spiritually along with teaching them.

in wine. Tannins are what cause that dry, puckery feeling in your mouth similar to biting into a green pear. Tannins are more present in red wines than whites, and they impede one's ability to taste.

"The other thing that strikes me," Kristof continued, "is that the story gives me a greater appreciation for winemaking in ancient times. Knowing the difficulty of making fine wine, even with all our modern technology and science, it's easy for me to discount the perceived quality of wine consumed in biblical times. I just kind of assumed it was a simple-tasting drink. But for the headwaiter to acknowledge the hosts' wine selection implies a high level of sophistication of the people and their palates in those times, which gives even more weight to the role of vineyards and winemaking in various passages."

Turning water into wine wasn't Jesus' only miracle involving food or beverage.

> **Read Matthew 14:14-21. What do the stories of Jesus turning water into wine and feeding five thousand have in common?**

> **What do they both reveal about Jesus?**

JUST BENEATH THE SURFACE

Intrigued by the wonder of the valley, I asked Kristof if we could see the vineyard. We followed him back down the spiral staircase and out a side door where gravel paths greeted us. Red-stone walls wound around the various flowering plants.

Land in Napa is nothing you can afford to waste, and the edge of the vineyard was only a stone's throw from the front door. The vineyard stretched down a slope before leveling across the plain. Each row revealed a stout, L–shaped vine that looked perfect for kindling. Planted equidistant from each other, the vines simply reached up from the earth with a solo branch running parallel to the ground. All other signs of growth had been removed.

"It looks dead," I said.

"You should see it in four weeks," Kristof pushed back. "You wouldn't recognize this vine—it will be so green and alive."

I brushed my fingers against the dry, flaky bark and struggled to imagine this vine containing any life.

"Let me show you," Kristof said, pulling out a pocketknife. He carefully scraped one of the nubs on an offshoot of the vine until a light green bud appeared.

"But it looks so dead," I pressed. "If this wasn't a vine in your care and you stumbled upon it in a random field, would you know whether it was alive or dead just from looking at it?"

"I wouldn't know," Kristof admitted. "You have to go below the surface to tell."

Have you ever viewed a situation or someone as "dead" only to discover that a lot was going on beneath the surface? What were the circumstances?

Have there been times in your own life when you appeared "dead" to others though a lot was going on beneath the surface?

Why do you think it's important to be wary of judging situations or people based on mere appearance?

R

Cultivating a vineyard takes a significant investment of time, money, and energy. To learn more, read section 4.5, "Long-Term Investment," in the *Scouting the Divine* book.

"Do not look at his appearance or at the height of his stature, because I have rejected him; for God sees not as man sees, for man looks at the outward appearance, but the LORD looks at the heart" (1 Samuel 16:7).

Jesus teaches us to be very careful about focusing on the surface and judging a situation based on sight:

"Do not judge so that you will not be judged. For in the way you judge, you will be judged; and by your standard of measure, it will be measured to you. Why do you look at the speck that is in your brother's eye, but do not notice the log that is in your own eye? Or how can you say to your brother, 'Let me take the speck out of your eye,' and behold, the log is in your own eye? You hypocrite, first take the log out of your own eye, and then you will see clearly to take the speck out of your brother's eye. Do not give what is holy to dogs, and do not throw your pearls before swine, or they will trample them under their feet, and turn and tear you to pieces" (Matthew 7:1-6).

Yet only a few verses later in Matthew 7:15-20, Jesus appears to teach the opposite, encouraging us to discern and examine the fruits of someone's life:

"Beware of the false prophets, who come to you in sheep's clothing, but inwardly are ravenous wolves. You will know them by their fruits. Grapes are not gathered from thorn bushes nor figs from thistles, are they? So every good tree bears good fruit, but the bad tree bears bad fruit. A good tree cannot produce bad fruit, nor can a bad tree produce good fruit. Every tree that does not bear good fruit is cut down and thrown into the fire. So then, you will know them by their fruits."

Do these two sections of Scripture contradict each other? Why or why not?

What is the major principle from each passage?

How should you handle the issue of judging others based on these Scriptures?

"Most of us are umpires at heart; we like to call balls and strikes on somebody else."[18]
—Leo Aikman, writer and newspaper editor

References to false prophets exist elsewhere in Scripture, too. Take a look at Deuteronomy 13:1-11 to see what the Old Testament has to say about them.

What other Scriptures come to mind as you reflect on this topic?

Do you think it's possible to wisely discern without being judgmental? How?

Another passage in Matthew that asserts the responsibility of the Christian community to exercise discipline and judgment comes in Matthew 18:15-20. This passage is the basis on which most congregations form their practice of church discipline.

One way to wisely discern is found in Matthew 7:1-5. The Scripture links the idea of judging to the way we are judged. It suggests that we can't begin the process of seeing what the issue really is (much less offering help) until we've dealt with the issues in our own hearts and lives. After we've dealt with our own issues—like a plank in the eye, which is painful, obtrusive, and uncomfortable—then we are in a better place to help others deal with their issues. We'll not only be able to see clearly, but we'll have compassion as we help them.

"We evaluate others with a Godlike justice, but we want them to evaluate us with a Godlike compassion," according to journalist Sydney J. Harris.[19]

VINES, WINES, AND THE BIBLE

Like sheep and shepherds, vines and vineyards provide a backdrop to some of Scripture's most memorable stories. While in a vineyard, Balaam and his donkey encountered an angel (Numbers 22:23-25). Elijah's fiery showdown with the prophets of Baal took place on top of Mount Carmel, a place that's name can be translated "vineyard of God" (1 Kings 18).

The prophet Isaiah portrayed Israel as God's vineyard (Isaiah 5:1-2), a land and people that He not only loves but has gone to great lengths to plant, cultivate, and protect. Like the image of God as a shepherd, the description of God as a vintner is one that implies a great investment of time, energy, and care. It also implies the expectation and promise of a fruitful and abundant harvest.

To read more about the fiery showdown on Mount Carmel between Elijah and the false prophets, read 1 Kings 18:16-45.

Have you ever imagined yourself as a vine in God's vineyard? What appeals to you about that image? What is difficult about that image?

How does this image change or add depth to the way you understand yourself and God?

If God's people are compared to a vineyard, it shouldn't be a surprise that at times the Bible refers to the vineyard or the fruit of the vine as unfruitful (Isaiah 5:2) or rotting (Hosea 10:1). The prophet Jeremiah uncovered Israel's estrangement to God by exposing their pursuit of worthless idols and their efforts at self-preservation. God Himself observed, "Yet I planted you a choice vine, a completely faithful seed. How then have you turned yourself before Me into the degenerate shoots of a foreign vine?" (Jeremiah 2:21).

Have you ever made decisions that ended up making you feel like "a foreign vine"? What does that phrase mean to you?

Vines and vineyards are sacred images in Judaism. The vine often represented God's people who were being tended by God to produce fruit. The vineyard image is popular throughout ancient Jewish literature.

The prophets often drew on the image of a vineyard producing bad grapes in order to paint a portrait of God's judgment (Jeremiah 5:10; Hosea 2:12; Amos 4:10). In the case of a vineyard continuing to produce bad grapes year after year, the vinedresser did everything possible to grow a good crop. But ultimately, if the vine only produced bad fruit, then the vinedresser had no choice but to destroy it and plant a new vineyard (Isaiah 5:5-7).

Scripture includes another reference to the judgment of God related to the vineyard, but in a slightly different context. In Deuteronomy, God gave the instruction that those who broke His laws could plant a vineyard but not enjoy the fruit (Deuteronomy 28:30,39). In this case, though the vineyard produced good fruit, judgment is pictured as the inability of the people to enjoy the harvest.

Zephaniah was a prophet during the reign of King Josiah, one of the last good kings of Judah. Zephaniah's great grandfather was Hezekiah, meaning that the prophet was cousin to King Josiah.

Zephaniah drew on this image when he proclaimed that the people of God wouldn't be able to enjoy the fruit of their labors because of their sin (Zephaniah 1:13). This prophecy was both figurative and literal, since military invasions often resulted in the destruction of agricultural production for a community. It was not uncommon for enemies to plunder and destroy the crops of the conquered land.

SESSION FIVE *SCOUTING THE DIVINE*

Have you ever been in a situation where you or someone you know couldn't enjoy the fruit of their labor? What specifically does a situation like that feel like?

Why do you think enjoying the fruit of your labor is part of God's blessing and reward?

While the loss of the vineyard is a sign of judgment, fruitfulness is a sign of God's restoration and redemption as well as His promise and blessing. Scripture reveals that when God chooses to restore and prosper His people, the sign of that blessing includes healthy vineyards (Amos 9:14). Nevertheless, Scripture is quick to forbid the abuse of wine and drunkenness (Ephesians 5:17-18).

The abuse of this enjoyment provides some of the most colorful illustrations of foolishness in the Bible. Though vines were most likely found in the garden, the first time a vineyard is mentioned is after the flood. Noah, described as a man of the soil, was probably not the founder of viticulture, but he certainly appreciated its fruits. After emerging from the ark, one of his first courses of action was to plant a vineyard. He foolishly drank the wine. A lot of it. His youngest son, Ham (the father of Canaan), found him passed out in his tent—naked—and rather than do something about it himself, he told his two brothers. Shem and Japheth chose to walk into the tent backward to cover up their father without looking at his nakedness (Genesis 9:20-27).

Why do you think the Bible warns so strongly against drunkenness?

Can you think of anything else that is meant to be enjoyed and yet dangerous when abused? Is there an overarching life principle true about all such things?

Make a Grape Juice Fizzle. Combine two cups of grape juice with one cup of club soda. Add a few slices of lime or lemon and some crushed ice. Enjoy!

In the DVD teaching segment for this session, Margaret is wearing a beaded necklace. Each bead is hand-crafted from scraps of newspaper and magazines by women in Africa. To learn more about the organization producing this jewelry, check out *comeletsdance.org.*

When Noah discovered what his youngest son had done (or left undone), he cursed Ham's descendents, the future Canaanites, to be the lowest of slaves. One of the particularly interesting (and depressing) things about this story is that Noah—who had himself had a first-hand encounter with God's grace when God promised to never again destroy the earth with rain—cursed part of his own family (Genesis 9:20-27).

Drunkenness brings out the worst in God's people. Lot committed incest with his daughters while drunk (Genesis 19:30-38), and the kings Amnon (2 Samuel 13:28) and Ben-hadad (1 Kings 20:16) were killed while they were drunk. King David tried to get Uriah drunk to cover up the whole Bathsheba incident (2 Samuel 11:13). Leaders who drink too much often compromise justice and morality (Isaiah 5:22). Proverbs warns listeners to stay away from drunkenness and all the foolish delusions and decisions that come with it (Proverbs 23:29-35).

Yet despite these clear warnings to stay away from drunkenness, the Bible draws on the image of the vineyard as a place of provision and blessing. When Jacob blessed his two sons, Judah and Joseph, he described Judah as tying his donkey to the best branches of a vine and having his robes washed in grape juice (Genesis 49:11). Meanwhile Joseph is described as a fruitful vine (Genesis 49:22). This particular description is intriguing because a vine was also part of the dream of the chief cupbearer, which Joseph interpreted (Genesis 40:8-14). It was that interpretation that eventually led to Joseph's rise to power in Egypt.

Draw a picture of a fruitful vine in the space below.

What are some of the characteristics of a fruitful vine? Which of those characteristics do you see God developing in your own life right now?

In the New Testament, the vineyard isn't as much a symbol of Israel as it is a representation of the kingdom of God. Jesus repeatedly wove vineyards and vines into His stories, and in one of His most well-known

More than 13,000 people die each year in DUI (driving under the influence) related accidents. It's estimated that 3 in every 10 Americans will be involved in an alcohol-related crash at some time in their lives. One such wreck occurs every 45 minutes, meaning by the time you finish this lesson, two people will have died.[20]

"One of life's gifts is that each of us, no matter how tired and downtrodden, finds reasons for thankfulness: for the crops carried in from the fields and the grapes from the vineyard."[21]
—J. Robert Moskin

teachings described Himself as the vine (John 15:1). He invited us to remain in Him in order to produce fruit. Jesus even used the fruit of the vine on the evening of His arrest as part of the final supper and meal that His followers are told to repeat in remembrance of Him (Matthew 26:26-30). These were the kinds of passages I couldn't wait to unpack with Kristof.

Select one of the passages mentioned in this overview of the roles of the vine and wine in the Bible. Read it aloud. Does anything from the passage surprise you?

Why do you think God used the theme of vines and vineyards throughout the Bible?

OUR GOD'S TENDER CARE

Throughout the Bible, the land and its produce are often used to illustrate and illuminate spiritual truths. This is particularly true of the use of vines, vineyards, and wine throughout Scripture. Jesus' first miracle was turning water into wine, a foreshadowing of the wedding feast that will come at the end of time. The careful process of growing and cultivating grapes can be a reflection of God's careful, tender care of each of us. Vines also remind us that sometimes there's more going on than first meets the eye, and in season healthy vines yield a harvest of fruit.

Lord, You truly are the One in whom we live, and move, and find our being. You're more intricately involved in our lives and in our world than we can ever comprehend. At times, we all doubt and feel bewildered at what You're doing, but the portrait of the vineyard reminds us that You're constantly at work—cultivating, nurturing, and creating something in and through us that we can't on our own. Give us eyes to see You in a fresh light. Give us ears to hear the ways You may be nudging us to grow, change, or even cut back. And give us hearts that are quickly responsive to You so that in season we may yield a harvest for You. In Jesus' name, amen.

R

To learn more about new versus old wineskins, read section 4.12, "New Wineskins," in the *Scouting the Divine* book.

Go online and share one thing you learned from this session using #scoutingthedivine.

ACTIVITY

Visit a local farmer's market or organic grocery store and buy a variety of grapes. If they carry any unusual varieties, go ahead and buy them. You may be surprised by what you find—table grapes, globe grapes, and even champagne grapes. Have each member of your group take samples from each of the varieties. Encourage them to take note of the wonderful differences in size, color, texture, and flavor in each one.

SCRIPTURE MEMORY

"Can a fig tree, my brethren, produce olives, or a vine produce figs? Nor can salt water produce fresh. Who among you is wise and understanding? Let him show by his good behavior his deeds in the gentleness of wisdom" (James 3:12-13).

SCOUTING THE DIVINE

As you go through the upcoming week, pay attention to everything you see that grows out of the ground. Take special note of any flowers, vines, shrubs, or trees you see. Think about what goes into keeping them alive. How is God working behind the scenes to make sure the vegetation lives a healthy, vibrant life? How are people working to ensure the vegetation lives a healthy, vibrant life? How much care goes into a single blade of grass, an old oak tree, or a patch of wildflowers? How much more care and attention goes into you?

SESSION
6

WITHIN THE VINE

Finding Ourselves in God

Kristof exhibited an unmistakable attentiveness when it came to the Bible. Though he never used them, he brought an Eastern Orthodox book on prayer and an Orthodox commentary for our conversation on Scripture.

I first pointed Kristof to a tucked away passage in the Old Testament where God instructed the Israelites about what would happen when they entered the promised land. In that land, they would enjoy cities they didn't build, houses full of good things they didn't buy, water from cisterns they didn't dig, and fruit from vineyards and olive trees they didn't plant. God warned them to be careful not to forget the Lord who brought them out of Egypt, the land of slavery (Deuteronomy 8:7-18). I asked Kristof if there's any correlation between the promised land inheritance and what people find when they move to the valley.

He explained that few people who inherit property in Napa and Sonoma are children of those who planted the vineyards. Most had parents who purchased the vineyards and then passed them on in their wills. All too often the inheritors end up disagreeing with what to do with the vineyard—with at least one person always wanting to sell—and the vineyard ends up being bought by a commercial company. A common problem among those who decide to keep their vineyards is that they lack the strong work ethic, passions, or abilities of their parents.

Not only did the Sabbath Year provide a period of rest for the land, it also foreshadowed a time in the future of prolonged rest and release from debt.

The "spiritual disciplines" are practices commanded and described in Scripture in order to help a person grow more mature in his or her relationship with Jesus. Some of the classic disciplines include prayer, fasting, Scripture memory, and meditation.

Another practical reason for the specific laws concerning the Sabbath Year was to prevent the formation of a class of rich landowners and a completely separate class of poor debtors.

Kristof's observations illuminated the idea that as the land was being passed down, there was a growing loss of appreciation for all they'd been given and all the work that had gone into the land. I couldn't help but see the parallel to passages of Scripture in Deuteronomy.

When things go wrong in life, it's easy to blame God and get mad at Him. But when things go right in life, it's even easier to forget God altogether. God knows this. In part, that's why He commanded the Israelites to remember Him and gave them specific instructions throughout the Torah (the first five books of the Old Testament) to help them remember. One of those instructions regarded the idea of scheduling regular times of rest and restoration in the form of a Sabbath.

What kind of days cause you to forget God?

What activities or possessions tempt you into living a life completely disconnected from God?

Which spiritual disciplines can help you live a more balanced life that remembers God in all you do?

One of the passages from the Old Testament that I was particularly interested in was a specific instruction found in Exodus, which said that every seventh year the land should rest and lie fallow. The Scripture is specific in saying, "You are to do the same with your vineyard and your olive grove" (Exodus 23:11). Apparently, God wanted to ensure the land, too, had a time of Sabbath rest.

When God spoke to Moses at Mount Sinai, He spoke directly about this issue:

"The LORD then spoke to Moses at Mount Sinai, saying, 'Speak to the sons of Israel and say to them, "When you come into the land which I shall give you, then the land shall have a sabbath to the LORD. Six years you shall sow your field, and six years you shall prune your vineyard and gather in its crop, but during the seventh year the land shall have a sabbath rest, a sabbath to the LORD; you shall not sow your field nor prune your vineyard.

Your harvest's aftergrowth you shall not reap, and your grapes of untrimmed vines you shall not gather; the land shall have a sabbatical year. All of you shall have the sabbath products of the land for food; yourself, and your male and female slaves, and your hired man and your foreign resident, those who live as aliens with you. Even your cattle and the animals that are in your land shall have all its crops to eat"' " (Leviticus 25:1-7).

> Why do you think God gave these specific commands regarding the land to Moses?

> How do you think the people benefited? How did the land benefit? The animals?

> What kind of planning do you think went into preparing for a Sabbath Year?

Though I had gently touched on this theme with Lynne in regard to the sheep, I wanted to ask Kristof because the Scripture seemingly went out of its way to mention the vineyards.

Kristof explained that while it's harder than ever for vintners to follow this advice, the longer you leave a parcel fallow the better it is for the

Watch the teaching segment "Finding Ourselves in God" from the *Scouting the Divine* DVD to see Margaret describe the God of the vine. You can watch the video during your *Scouting the Divine* study group or download it for yourself at margaretfeinberg.com.

While seven-day periods of time were well known in the ancient Near East and even addressed in literature, Israel was unique in that it set apart the seventh day for rest.

"A person who feels inclined to work seven days a week should examine what god he or she worships... Those who find their security and significance in mammon or professionalism find community worship on the first day of the week a burden."[22] —Bruce K. Waltke, Old Testament scholar next vineyard you plant. Since the vines are taking nutrients out of the soil, the longer you don't plant vines, the more the soil can restore itself. This is true not only when you plant a new vineyard but also between series of harvests.

> **How do you think you can integrate this principle of fallowness and Sabbath into your everyday life?**

> **How willing are you to allow areas of your life to lie fallow? Does this practice come easily for you? Why or why not?**

In Exodus 20, the Fourth of the Ten Commandments calls us to rest. This command is grounded in creation, when God worked for six days and rested on the seventh. Read the whole account in Genesis 1:1–2:3.

In Jewish custom, Sabbath was observed on the seventh day of the week, beginning at sundown on Friday and ending at sundown on Saturday.

"The downtime allows the soil of the vineyard to regain the nitrogen it needs to produce a delicious harvest," he explained.

"So the grapes taste better?" I asked.

"Yes."

Unknowingly, Kristof had touched on something I was learning in my own spiritual life—just as the land needed a Sabbath, I did, too. During the last two months, Leif and I had been on the road traveling, teaching, and researching. Most of the commitments were made more than a year before, long before we'd learned to calculate recovery time into our travels. The result was a series of go-go-go obligations without any chance to stop, rest, or recover. Not only did I find myself catching every strain of flu that went around because of a weak immune system, but I also struggled with irritability, overeating, and over-reacting. I felt discombobulated and out of balance. As we were nearing the end of our busy time, I discovered something else: The sweet moments of life lost their sweetness and the sharp moments of life became more bitter.

And maybe this was the greatest loss of all. Life without the gift of rest decreases our ability to enjoy the bouquet of all we've been given. Just as the fruit of Kristof's vines eventually suffered without respite, so too did the fruit of my own life.

Have you ever repeatedly ignored or chosen to skip the command to rest on a regular basis? What was the result?

Have you ever practiced keeping the Sabbath on a regular basis? What differences did you notice in your life? Specifically, were there any differences in your attitude? Your affection toward God?

Why do you think honoring the Sabbath is so difficult in our culture?

If you're interested in learning more about the Sabbath and incorporating the practice into your life, pick up a copy of *The Rest of God* by Mark Buchanan.

Jesus tells us in Mark 2:27 that the weekly Sabbath (and by implication the seventh year rest of the land) is meant for humanity. The act of stopping work has a way of realigning our priorities. In the process of practicing the Sabbath, we are reminded that God is ultimately our Provider. When we Sabbath, we reveal God to truly be Lord of our lives and acknowledge that we won't be ruled by lesser desires or false gods.

"Observance of the Sabbath by man is thus a confession that Yahweh is Lord and Lord of all lords. Sabbath-keeping expresses man's commitment to the service of the Lord."[23]
—M. G. Kline, author

The Sabbath invites us to a time of connecting with God, studying Scripture, and reflecting on His presence in our lives. In the New Testament we get a glimpse of this practice as religious leaders read, wrestled, and even argued the Scriptures on the Sabbath (as found in Mark 1:21; Luke 4:16-20; and Acts 13:13-45).

Practicing the Sabbath was originally designed for Israel, but everyone living among the Israelites—slave and free, and even their animals—benefited from the practice and enjoyed a time of rest. Sabbath is a gift not only to God's people but to all people through them. The rabbis perverted God's gift by adding rules and regulations to the Sabbath, thus making it difficult for the people to enjoy. This is one reason Jesus often defended the Sabbath and repeatedly demonstrated to the people that the Sabbath was a time of doing good and healing (Matthew 12:1-14; Mark 2:23-28).

When we choose to practice the Sabbath, we discover new depths of God's provision, including refreshment and renewal, and place ourselves in the best possible position to share it with others. The vineyard and the enjoyment it promises for others serves as a powerful reminder of this basic truth.

> In your opinion, what is the most appealing part of practicing the Sabbath?

> How would practicing the Sabbath lead you to share the enjoyment of God's provision with others?

In this proverb, verses 10-31 are an acrostic. Every verse begins with a different Hebrew letter, going through the entire Hebrew alphabet in order.

THE IDEAL WOMAN

I was curious as to Kristof's perspective of Proverbs 31. This chapter of Scripture describes what has often been called "the ideal woman." According to Proverbs, one of the many things this woman does in her free time is buy a field and plant a vineyard (Proverbs 31:16-17). This passage is intriguing because it follows some strong words a mother gave her son about avoiding strong drink (Proverbs 23). Overindulgence leads to poor decisions about women and life, as well as a numbness regarding care for the poor. This contrasts sharply with the Proverbs 31 woman, who is specifically commended for her business acumen and care for those less fortunate than her.

> Read Proverbs 31:10-31 *aloud*. Take a few moments to interact with this passage. First, go through the Scripture and circle all of the verbs. Then double underline all of the adjectives used to describe this woman.

On a scale from 1 to 10, how busy and active is the woman described? What does that indicate to you about her character and priorities?

What are the most surprising or intriguing adjectives you found? Regardless of your gender, place a star by the adjectives you'd like people to use to describe you.

🎧

Listen to the audio segment "Meet Kristof the Vintner" this week. Your group leader will send it to you via e-mail, or you can download it at *margaretfeinberg.com*. These audio recordings are designed to help you connect more deeply with God the Vintner as you spend time Scouting the Divine.

As I read the final chapter of Proverbs aloud to Kristof, I noticed that of all the places this woman could have selected to invest her time and money, she chose a vineyard.

"Why?" I asked abruptly. "From your perspective, what's going through her mind?"

"She's resourceful for sure," Kristof said. "But there's something more. Anyone who plants a vineyard is looking ahead to the future. She has the foresight to know that it's going to be three to four years before she sees any fruit—literally or figuratively—from her labor. She also knows that for the next 50 years, she and her family are going to get fruit, and even if it's not for wine, she's still thinking long term. If you're only thinking for the here and now, you'd plant a different crop."

📺

In the teaching segment for Session Six, the puppy beside Margaret in the vineyard is her dog, Hershey. He weighs in between four and five pounds. Yes, he's smaller than most people's cats.

As I thought more about it, her foresight became even more obvious. Throughout the Old Testament, the image of growing a vineyard is one of stability, financial prosperity, and longevity. Maybe the Proverbs 31 woman knew that in his wisdom, Solomon, too, had planted vineyards (Ecclesiastes 2:4). It would take plenty of work, and I'm sure some sleepless nights, but her investment would pay dividends to her family for years to come.

Do you tend to view life from a short-term perspective or a long-term perspective? What are some of the benefits of thinking long-term (relationally, spiritually, financially, etc.)?

What choices are you making today that will affect future generations? Specifically, how will your choices today affect your own children, nieces, or nephews?

What other lessons can you learn from the Proverbs 31 woman's commitment to the vineyard?

Listen to "Hope Now" by Addison Road from the *Scouting the Divine* playlist. Your group leader can e-mail you the whole playlist, or you can download it at *margaretfeinberg.com*.

ABIDING IN THE VINE

Kristof and I talked about various passages that touch on the themes of vines and vineyards, but one that I couldn't wait to get to was John 15. Similar to John 10 where Jesus used the image of the shepherd as a description of His life, work, and relationship with us, John 15 records Jesus' use of the image of a vineyard as a colorful metaphor for living in relationship with God.

It's interesting to note that John 15:1 is the final "I am" saying of Jesus in the Gospel of John. Jesus boldly declared, "I am the true vine." But there are six other "I am" statements found within the Book of John.

In the lists below, match the passage with the statement.

Scripture	Statement
John 6:35	Light of the World
John 8:12	The Way, the Truth, and the Life
John 10:7	Bread of Life
John 10:11-14	The Good Shepherd
John 11:25	The Door
John 14:6	The Resurrection and the Life

Do you think there's anything significant about the order in which Jesus reveals Himself through the "I am" statements? Why or why not?

Of all the "I am" statements, which one is most descriptive of your relationship with Jesus? Which is least descriptive?

Read John 15:1-8 *aloud*. Reading through the passage in which Jesus compared Himself to the vine, Kristof noted that it was quite an analogy. I asked him to look at the passage line by line through the lens of a vintner.

Reflecting on Jesus' opening statement, "I am the true vine, and My Father is the vinedresser," Kristof released a warm "hmmm" sound before declaring, "I love this verse. What's interesting is that the passage doesn't identify the full role of His Father," he observed.

I was confused. The passage clearly said that the Father was the vinedresser. "What do you mean?" I pressed.

"In a vineyard, people often have multiple roles, and the Father probably isn't just the vinedresser—He plays a role as the owner of the vineyard, the manager of the vineyard, and the vintner, too," Kristof said. "But of all the titles, Jesus gives His Father the title of vinedresser, and that's the one pruning or sculpting the vine."

Why was the role of vinedresser so important? Why didn't Jesus give the Father the title of owner? It seemed to me that owner would be a title of greater honor and prominence. Why did Jesus choose this particular title for the Father in His teaching? While Scripture doesn't explicitly say, Kristof had an intriguing observation: "It may surprise you, but whoever is pruning a vine really is the master. Even in our vineyards, the owner may possess the land, and I might be making the wine, but it's the guy making $12 an hour with the shears who has all the power."

Branches are trimmed from a vine for two reasons. First, they are removed so the vine can produce even more fruit. Second, the dead branches that have no life and get in the way are removed. Real fruit-bearing only comes with the life-giving connection to the vine.

Does it surprise you that the vinedresser is actually more powerful than the owner of the vineyard? Why do you think that person has all the power?

Do you tend to think of God as the vinedresser, owner of the vineyard, or both? Explain.

The Greek word for "trimming" (*kathario*) is closely related to the word translated "clean" (*katharos*) found in John 15:3. It's interesting that the idea of pruning and cleaning would be so intimately linked.

Kristof continued reading aloud, "Every branch in Me that does not bear fruit, He takes away; and every branch that bears fruit, He prunes it so that it may bear more fruit."

Pushing his chair back from the desk, he balanced for a moment on the back two legs. He explained that as a kid when he read that passage, he always thought the practice of pruning was easy.

"I thought you'd just walk up to a vine, see a branch with fruit, and say, 'We'll keep that one,'" Kristof reflected. "You'd see another branch without fruit and cut it off. But as a vintner there's a lot more decision making and expertise going on in this passage than appears at first glance."

"What do you mean?" I asked.

"It's the little cuts which are the most impactful," he explained. "You can't come in with a pair of shears and clip like crazy. You don't just look at what appears to be a dead branch and cut it off and then look at a branch full of fruit and think it's fine. But over the course of pruning, you make a series of very precise, strategic cuts that will produce the healthiest, most robust vine."

"Which highlights just how intimately involved God is in our lives," I interjected.

"And also how God handles each of us differently," Kristof added.

One of the most recognizable places in Scripture where we see the metaphor of "fruit" is in Galatians 5. In that chapter, Paul contrasted the fruit of the Spirit with the works of the flesh.

I asked him to clarify. He explained that if a vinedresser chooses the wrong cuts, the vine won't produce fruit. That's why a vinedresser looks at each vine carefully. Every vine is unique. Even two vines planted next to each other may require significantly different small cuts in order to produce fruit.

"One vine may have great soil and be strong enough to handle a significant pruning, but the next vine may be weaker and the same pruning would leave it fruitless," he explained.

"Which may be one more reason Jesus chose to describe His Father as vinedresser," I offered. "He's the only one who can make those judgments."

Do you tend to view God's pruning in your life as one or two huge cuts or a series of small cuts that shape you into the fullness of who He is creating you to be? Why?

Which do you think is more effective? Which do you prefer?

How does having a healthy perspective on pruning help you grow to your full potential? How does having an unhealthy perspective on pruning limit your ability to grow to your full potential?

Kristof described two vines next to each other that may need completely different care from the vinedresser. Have you ever looked at someone else's life and wondered why they've had a completely different experience with God than you? If so, describe.

"My son, do not reject the discipline of the LORD or loathe His reproof, for whom the LORD loves He reproves, even as a father corrects the son in whom he delights" (Proverbs 3:11-12).

What does it mean to "abide in Christ"? The literal translation of "abide" is to remain or dwell. However, the word can also be translated as "to stand firm or steadfast." Abiding, then, has a definite sense of perseverance in difficulty associated with it.

Andrew Murray's classic *Abide in Christ* remains one of the best and most lasting descriptions of what it means to truly live for and in God. Pick up a copy soon.

To learn more about the four cups of Passover, read section 4.14, "Until That Day," in the *Scouting the Divine* book.

I nudged Kristof forward in the text to the invitation of Jesus to abide in Him. I read John 15:4 slowly, "As the branch cannot bear fruit of itself unless it abides in the vine, so neither can you unless you abide in Me."

Kristof didn't hesitate to respond. "If you cut off a branch and expect it to bear fruit on its own without a root structure or nutrients and water, it will simply wither up and die. The vine is the source of life. In the abiding, the fruit grows."

"But what about Jesus' claim that anyone who does not abide in Him will be thrown away, dry up, and eventually be burned?" I asked.

The description wasn't just figurative but literal. "After the branches are pruned they are gathered and burned," Kristof explained. "Today because of air quality concerns we don't burn all of them anymore, but the old-timers always burned what was pruned."

I felt an unmistakable sense of comfort and hope in Kristof's observation. A hope that God will prune away our sin and the unhealthy parts of us and destroy those things so that we grow even more full, healthy, and vibrant.

Does thinking about pruning make you desire God's pruning process in your life more or less?

What do you find to be the most difficult part of the pruning process?

What role does faith play in accepting pruning from God?

John 15:7 was the verse that seemed to stump Kristof: "If you abide in Me, and My words abide in you, ask whatever you wish, and it will be done for you."

"That one has always bothered me," Kristof admitted, "because I've seen people use the promise to 'ask whatever you wish' to do some pretty ludicrous and even abusive things."

"I have too," I agreed. "But being here with you and walking the vines gives me hope in Jesus' words."

"How so?" he asked.

"Because the vines, your vines, are a perfect portrait of abiding. The vine is the source of everything for the branch—every nutrient, every life-giving drop of water, every hint of growth—so the branch is completely dependent on the vine. But even in those moments when I grow wild or unbalanced, God is faithful as a vinedresser to perform all the small cuts I need to remain fruitful. In that place where I am abiding in Christ under the watchful eye of the Father, the things I ask for will naturally be rooted in all God has planted and created me to be."

KEEPER OF THE VINE

My time with the vintner taught me something about the paradox of pruning that deep down I didn't really want to know—to grow we must be cut back. Just as the vine can't produce quality grapes year-round, neither can we expect to be fruitful all day, every day. Though painful, pruning is one of God's greatest acts of love. Through the vintner I discovered God as the keeper of the vine—One who protects and nurtures us so we can bear the fruit He has set out for us to produce.

Lord, You are the keeper of all things—including us. We ask that You give us the courage to fully submit ourselves to You. We ask that You would spotlight those areas in our lives that need to be cut back. Those areas where we need to learn to say no. Those areas of deadness that really must go. Illuminate those areas with Your Spirit and with Your loving touch; prune them from our lives so we may learn to abide wholly, fully, completely undistracted in You. Help us to recognize those things in life—busyness, apathy, bitterness—that separate us from You and make it impossible to remain fully in You. Give us the grace to make wise choices and loving friends to celebrate our journeys with You every step of the way. We are grateful to be Your children and share Your love with those who don't know You yet. In Jesus' name, amen.

"For by Him all things were created, both in the heavens and on earth, visible and invisible, whether thrones or dominions or rulers or authorities—all things have been created through Him and for Him. He is before all things, and in Him all things hold together" (Colossians 1:16-17).

Drop a note to Margaret sharing how this study has impacted you. E-mail her at *hello@margaretfeinberg. com.* She'll be thrilled to hear from you.

ACTIVITY

Whether it's indoors or outdoors, plant something that requires pruning. Consider planting a few perennials, a rose bush, or even some raspberries. Then spend some time researching what pruning that particular plant requires. Almost every type of plant is different, and pruning too much at the wrong time of year can not only diminish fruitfulness but on rare occasions hurt the plant. Share what you learn with your study group. As you learn more about pruning, consider the cutting back God may be doing in your life.

SCRIPTURE MEMORY

"I am the true vine, and My Father is the vinedresser. Every branch in Me that does not bear fruit, He takes away; and every branch that bears fruit, He prunes it so that it may bear more fruit" (John 15:1-2).

SCOUTING THE DIVINE

During the next week, reflect on what you've learned through this study. Revisit any notes you've taken. Refresh your memory with the various Scriptures you know by heart. And spend some time prayerfully reflecting on what you've discovered about God and Scripture through this study. Now begin Scouting the Divine on your own. Select one agricultural theme from the Bible and use a concordance to look up every place it's mentioned in Scripture (think about rain, drought, or trees to get you started). Read the verse and the surrounding context. Consider using a commentary or Bible reference tool to dig deeper. Then research online or spend time with someone who is involved in that particular agricultural practice. Ask God to make the truths of Scripture real in your life.

END NOTES

SESSION 1
1. John Calvin, *Institutes of the Christian Religion,* trans. Henry Beveridge (Peabody, Mass.: Hendrickson Publishers, Inc., 2008), 223.

SESSION 2
2. C. S. Lewis, *The Screwtape Letters* (New York: Harper Collins, 2001), 65.
3. *http://thinkexist.com/quotation/if_you_have_men_who_will_exclude_any_of_god-s/219105.html*
4. Roy B. Zuck, *The Speaker's Quote Book: Over 4,500 Illustrations and Quotations for All Occasions* (Grand Rapids: Kregel Publications, 1997), 400.
5. *http://thinkexist.com/quotation/there_is_only_one_thing_more_painful_than/221237.html*
6. *http://www.worldofquotes.com/proverb/Russian/4/index.html*
7. Charles R. Swindoll, *The Owner's Manual for Christians* (Nashville: Thomas Nelson, 2009), 97.

SESSION 3
8. *http://quickfacts.census.gov/qfd/states/31000.html* and *http://www.citypopulation.de/USA-NewYork.html*
9. Kenneth E. Bailey, *Jesus through Middle Eastern Eyes: Cultural Studies in the Gospels* (Downers Grove: Intervarsity Press, 2008), 302.
10. *http://quotationsbook.com/quote/4130/*
11. *http://thinkexist.com/quotation/i-do-not-at-all-understand-the-mystery-of-grace/761218.html*
12. *http://thinkexist.com/quotation/all_poetry_is_an_ordered_voice-one_which_tries_to/218073.html*

SESSION 4
13. For these and other bee facts, refer to the National Honey Board's Web site, *honey.com.*
14. *http://thinkexist.com/quotation/the_bee_is_more_honored_than_other_animals-not/196051.html*
15. ANI, "Oldest known archaeological example of beekeeping discovered in Israel," Thaindian News [online], 1 September 2008 [cited 15 October 2009]. Available from the Internet: *www.thaindian.com*
16. Lane T. Dennis, ed., *Letters of Francis A. Schaeffer* (Westchester, Ill: Crossway Books, 1985), 37.
17. *http://thinkexist.com/quotation/hope_is_the_only_bee_that_makes_honey_without/224560.html*

SESSION 5
18. *http://quotationsbook.com/quote/9235/*
19. *http://www.dailywisdom.com/dw_static/quotesall.html*
20. *http://www.madd.org/Drunk-Driving/Drunk-Driving/Statistics.aspx*
21. *http://thinkexist.com/quotes/j._robert_moskin/*

SESSION 6
22. Bruce K. Waltke, *Genesis: A Commentary* (Grand Rapids: Zondervan, 2001), 72.
23. M. G. Kline, *Kingdom Prologue* (Hamilton, Mass.: Meredith Kline, 1993), 25.

SCOUTING THE DIVINE

NOTES

SCRIPTURE MEMORY

"I am the good shepherd, and I know My own and My own know Me, even as the Father knows Me and I know the Father; and I lay down My life for the sheep."
(John 10:14-15)

"For You formed my inward parts; You wove me in my mother's womb. I will give thanks to You, for I am fearfully and wonderfully made; Wonderful are Your works, And my soul knows it very well."
(Psalm 139:13-14)

"Now the God of peace, who brought up from the dead the great Shepherd of the sheep through the blood of the eternal covenant, even Jesus our Lord, equip you in every good thing to do His will, working in us that which is pleasing in His sight, through Jesus Christ, to whom be the glory forever and ever. Amen."
(Hebrews 13:20-21)

"Can a fig tree, my brethren, produce olives, or a vine produce figs? Nor can salt water produce fresh. Who among you is wise and understanding? Let him show by his good behavior his deeds in the gentleness of wisdom."
(James 3:12-13)

"For I am confident of this very thing, that He who began a good work in you will perfect it until the day of Christ Jesus."
(Philippians 1:6)

"I am the true vine, and My Father is the vinedresser. Every branch in Me that does not bear fruit, He takes away; and every branch that bears fruit, He prunes it so that it may bear more fruit."
(John 15:1-2)

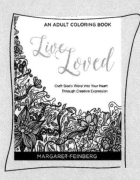

LIVE LOVED:
AN ADULT COLORING BOOK
Craft God's Word into Your Heart Through Creative Expression

How would your attitude, actions, and responses change if you lived in the unconditional, immeasurable love of God? How would your relationships with others be transformed if you invited the love of God to flow to and through you? What would it look like for you to live loved?

An adult coloring book designed for families and friends, *Live Loved* provides an opportunity for you to pull away from the hustle and bustle of life to pray, reflect, journal, and unleash your creative gifts as you marinate in the truth of God's fierce love for you.

LIVE FREE:
AN ADULT COLORING BOOK
Craft God's Word into Your Heart Through Creative Expression

Who am I? This is one of the most difficult questions we can ask ourselves, and we can spend a lifetime trying to answer it. Yet we can go straight to the Master Artist and ask God who He made us to be.

Live Free: An Adult Coloring Book provides an opportunity for you to pull away from the hustle and bustle of life to pray, journal, and unleash your creative gifts and discover your true identity.

LIVE FEARLESS:
AN ADULT COLORING BOOK
Craft God's Word into Your Heart Through Creative Expression

What if? Life is riddled with uncertainty. Perhaps that's why Jesus is so passionate in His command, "Do not fear." He challenges us to enter uncertainty with faith, the unknown with trust, the uncharted with hope.

Live Fearless: An Adult Coloring Book provides an opportunity for you to pull away from the hustle and bustle of life to pray, journal, and unleash your creative gifts and rediscover the goodness and faithfulness of God no matter what you're facing.

START COLORING TODAY:
MARGARETFEINBERG.COM

FIGHT BACK WITH JOY
Celebrate More. Regret Less. Stare Down Your Greatest Fears.
6-Session DVD Bible Study Kit

Through vulnerable storytelling, a difficult diagnosis, and a good dose of humor, *Fight Back With Joy* will help you expand your joy threshold by awakening to God's fierce love for you, escape fear and regret by applying biblical strategies to whatever crisis you're facing, overcome depression as you reignite your imagination for laughter and celebration, and rise above endless demands and become more winsome, cheerful, and thankful. Ranked one of the top 3 Bible studies of 2015 by Lifeway.

WONDERSTRUCK
Awaken to the Nearness of God
7-Session DVD Bible Study Kit

Through seven sessions filmed in the Canadian Rockies, *Wonderstruck* will help you renew your passion for God, discover peace in knowing your wildy loved, and recognize the presence of God.

Five nights of homework each week (20 min.) and the companion trade book, will help you discover how much God is busting at the seams to display His power, glory, and might in your life.

THE SACRED ECHO
Hearing God's Voice in Every Area of Your Life
6-Session DVD Bible Study Kit

Are you ready to revolutionize your prayer life forever? *The Sacred Echo* explores that when God speaks, He will echo the same message through a sermon, a passage of Scripture, a chance conversation, or an unexpected encounter. When we begin looking for these sacred echoes, we are better able to recognize God's voice in our life and walk more confidently in the fullness of all God has for us.

The workbook provides 20 minutes of homework each week and the companion trade book provides additional rich insights for participants.

**TO ORDER & WATCH VIDEO SAMPLES,
VISIT MARGARETFEINBERG.COM.**

ALSO AVAILABLE
WHEREVER BOOKS ARE SOLD

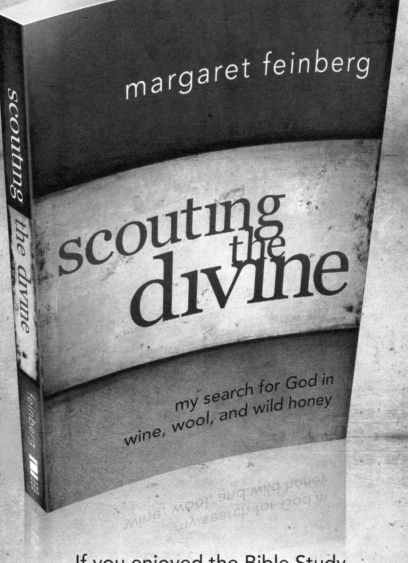

If you enjoyed the Bible Study, you'll love the book for yourself or to give to a friend or family member.

For more information, visit www.zondervan.com or www.margaretfeinberg.com

GROUP CONTACT INFORMATION

Name _____ Number _____
E-mail _____

Name _____ Number _____
E-mail _____

Name _____ Number _____
E-mail _____

Name _____ Number _____
E-mail _____

Name _____ Number _____
E-mail _____

Name _____ Number _____
E-mail _____

Name _____ Number _____
E-mail _____

Name _____ Number _____
E-mail _____

Name _____ Number _____
E-mail _____

Name _____ Number _____
E-mail _____